The Complete GOLO Diet Cookbook

Transform Your Health and Waistline with Flavorful, Satisfying Recipes Designed for Optimal Insulin Regulation and Weight Loss Success

Lara Meyer

PUBLISHED BY: Lara Meyer

©Copyright 2023 - All rights reserved.

All rights reserved. No part of this publication may be reproduced, distributed, or transmitted in any form or by any means, including photocopying, recording, or other electronic or mechanical methods, without the prior written permission of the publisher, except in the case of brief quotations embodied in critical reviews and certain other noncommercial uses permitted by copyright law.

Under no circumstances will any blame or legal responsibility be held against the publisher, or author, for any damages, reparation, or monetary loss due to the information contained within this book, either directly or indirectly.

Legal Notice:

This book is copyright protected. It is only for personal use. You cannot amend, distribute, sell, use, quote or paraphrase any part, or the content within this book, without the consent of the author or publisher.

Disclaimer Notice:

Please note the information contained within this document is for educational and entertainment purposes only. All effort has been executed to present accurate, up to date, reliable, complete information. No warranties of any kind are declared or implied. Readers acknowledge that the author is not engaged in the rendering of legal, financial, medical or professional advice. The content within this book has been derived from various sources. Please consult a licensed professional before attempting any techniques outlined in this book.

By reading this document, the reader agrees that under no circumstances is the author responsible for any losses, direct or indirect, that are incurred as a result of the use of the information contained within this document, including, but not limited to, errors, omissions, or inaccuracies.

Table of Contents

Introduction   1
   GOLO Diet: Overview and philosophy   1
   How the GOLO Diet Works   2

Getting Started with the GOLO Diet   4
   Preparing Your Kitchen   4
   Meal Planning and Preparation   6

Breakfast   9
   Green Smoothie   10
   Berry Protein Shake   11
   Veggie Omelette   12
   Egg Muffins   14
   Chia Seed Pudding   16
   Greek Yogurt Parfait   18
   Breakfast Quinoa Bowl   19
   Spinach and Mushroom Frittata   21
   Almond Flour Pancakes   23
   Coconut Flour Waffles   25
   Savory Oatmeal   26
   Shakshuka   28
   Overnight Oats   30
   Sweet Potato Hash   31

Broccoli and Cheese Egg Cups … 33
Banana Almond Smoothie … 35
Granola and Yogurt Bowl … 36
Vegetable Scramble … 37
Baked Oatmeal … 39
Quinoa Breakfast Porridge … 41

Lunch … 43

Greek Salad with Chicken … 44
Tuna Salad Lettuce Wraps … 46
Cauliflower Fried Rice … 48
Turkey and Avocado Sandwich … 50
Zucchini Noodle Salad … 52
Grilled Veggie Quinoa Bowl … 54
Shrimp and Asparagus Stir-Fry … 56
Chicken Fajita Salad … 58
Spinach and Quinoa Stuffed Peppers … 60
Tomato and Mozzarella Salad … 62
Broccoli and Chicken Stir-Fry … 63
Spaghetti Squash Pad Thai … 65
Roasted Vegetable Farro Salad … 67
Lentil Soup … 69
Chicken and Avocado Salad … 71
Turkey and Veggie Stuffed Pita … 73
Vegetable Chickpea Curry … 75
Cobb Salad … 77
Cauliflower and Chickpea Tacos … 79
Egg Salad Sandwich … 81

Dinner … 83

Grilled Chicken and Vegetables … 84
Baked Salmon and Asparagus … 86

Table of Contents

Beef and Broccoli Stir-Fry	88
Roasted Vegetable Quinoa	90
Turkey Meatballs with Zucchini Noodles	91
Chicken and Veggie Sheet Pan Dinner	93
Shrimp and Cauliflower Grits	95
Spinach and Feta Stuffed Chicken	97
Stuffed Portobello Mushrooms	99
Cilantro Lime Chicken and Rice	101
Eggplant Parmesan	103
Ground Turkey Lettuce Wraps	105
Black Bean and Sweet Potato Chili	107
Baked Cod with Tomatoes and Olives	109
Chicken, Mushroom, and Spinach Skillet	110
Slow Cooker Pulled Pork	111
Vegetable Stir-Fry with Tofu	112
Chicken Piccata	114
Pork Tenderloin with Roasted Vegetables	116
Seared Scallops with Cauliflower Puree	117
Snacks and Appetizers	**119**
Veggie Sticks with Hummus	120
Baked Kale Chips	121
Apple Slices with Almond Butter	122
Greek Salad Skewers	123
Spicy Roasted Chickpeas	124
Mini Caprese Bites	126
Zucchini Fritters	127
Smoked Salmon Cucumber Bites	129
Almond Stuffed Dates	130
Turkey and Cheese Roll-Ups	131
Baked Sweet Potato Fries	132

Guacamole with Bell Pepper Dippers — 134

Antipasto Skewers — 136

Deviled Eggs — 138

Side Dishes — 139

Garlic Green Beans — 140

Quinoa Pilaf — 141

Roasted Brussels Sprouts — 143

Grilled Asparagus — 144

Cauliflower Rice — 145

Balsamic Glazed Carrots — 146

Lemon Herb Couscous — 147

Cilantro Lime Rice — 149

Steamed Broccoli with Lemon — 151

Sweet and Spicy Roasted Butternut Squash — 152

Desserts and Sweet Treats — 153

Flourless Chocolate Cake — 154

Baked Applies with Cinnamon — 156

Coconut Macaroons — 157

Greek Yogurt with Honey and Nuts — 159

Mixed Berry Crumble — 160

Chocolate-Dipped Strawberries — 161

Almond Butter Cookies — 162

Frozen Banana Bites — 163

Pumpkin Mousse — 165

Fruit Salad with Lime and Mint — 166

Beverages — 167

Cucumber Mint Infused Water — 168

Green Tea with Lemon and Ginger — 169

Iced Coffee with Almond Milk — 170

Table of Contents

Strawberry and Basil Lemonade 171

Golden Milk Latte 172

Introduction

Welcome to a world of vibrant health, sustainable weight loss, and a renewed sense of well-being. As you embark on your journey with the GOLO Diet, you're not only embracing a new way of eating, but also a holistic lifestyle that aims to nourish both your body and mind. In this first chapter, we'll provide you with a comprehensive understanding of the GOLO Diet, its core principles, and the science behind its effectiveness. We'll guide you through the process of transforming your kitchen, planning nutritious meals, and developing mindful eating habits that will serve as the foundation for your new, healthier lifestyle. So, let's dive in and explore the power of the GOLO Diet, as we begin our journey towards a happier, healthier, and more vibrant you.

GOLO Diet: Overview and philosophy

The GOLO Diet is an innovative approach to weight loss and healthy living that focuses on balancing hormones, optimizing insulin levels, and promoting overall wellness. Its philosophy is rooted in the belief that the key to sustainable weight loss and improved health lies in addressing the root causes of weight gain and metabolic imbalances. By targeting insulin resistance, the GOLO Diet aims to help individuals achieve and maintain their ideal weight while also enhancing their overall well-being.

At the core of the GOLO Diet is the principle of "fueling metabolism," which emphasizes the importance of eating the right foods in the right quantities to optimize metabolic function. This is achieved through a combination of wholesome, nutrient-dense meals and a supportive supplement called Release, designed to further balance blood sugar levels and improve metabolic efficiency. The diet encourages mindful eating, portion control, and a focus on whole, unprocessed foods that are rich in nutrients, fiber, and healthy fats.

Health Benefits

The GOLO Diet offers a multitude of health benefits beyond weight loss. As the diet targets insulin resistance and balances blood sugar levels, it can help reduce the risk of developing type 2 diabetes, cardiovascular diseases, and other metabolic disorders. By promoting a nutrient-rich diet and discouraging the consumption of processed foods, the GOLO Diet also supports better digestion, increased energy levels, and improved mental clarity.

Additionally, the diet encourages a more balanced approach to food, discouraging restrictive and unsustainable eating habits. This focus on mindful eating and portion control can help individuals develop a healthier relationship with food, which can lead to long-term success in maintaining a healthy weight and lifestyle.

Weight Loss Approach

The GOLO Diet's weight loss approach is rooted in addressing insulin resistance, a common issue for many people struggling with weight loss. Insulin resistance occurs when cells in the body do not respond efficiently to insulin, leading to elevated blood sugar levels and, ultimately, weight gain. By balancing insulin levels, the GOLO Diet aims to improve metabolic function, allowing individuals to more effectively burn fat and lose weight.

How the GOLO Diet Works

Insulin Resistance and Weight Loss

The GOLO Diet focuses on combating insulin resistance, a key factor in weight gain and difficulty losing weight. Insulin is a hormone responsible for regulating blood sugar levels, and when cells become resistant to its effects, blood sugar levels rise. This can lead to weight gain and difficulty shedding excess pounds. By targeting insulin resistance, the GOLO Diet helps improve the body's ability to process sugars and burn fat more efficiently, promoting weight loss.

The role of metabolic fuel

Metabolic fuel is a crucial component of the GOLO Diet's weight loss strategy. The diet emphasizes the importance of consuming a balanced combination of proteins, fats, and carbohydrates to optimize metabolism and promote weight loss. The diet encourages the consumption of whole, unprocessed foods, such as lean proteins, healthy fats, and complex carbohydrates, which provide the necessary nutrients for efficient metabolic function. By fueling the metabolism with the right nutrients, the GOLO Diet helps the body burn fat more effectively and supports sustainable weight loss.

The importance of portion control and balanced meals

Portion control and balanced meals play an essential role in the success of the GOLO Diet. The diet encourages individuals to be mindful of their portion sizes and consume an appropriate amount of food for their specific needs. By practicing portion control, individuals can avoid overeating and maintain a healthy caloric intake, which is key to weight loss.

Balanced meals are also a critical aspect of the GOLO Diet. Meals should consist of a combination of proteins, fats, and carbohydrates, ensuring that the body receives the necessary nutrients for optimal metabolic function. Incorporating a variety of whole, unprocessed foods not only provides essential nutrients but also promotes satiety, helping individuals feel full and satisfied after meals. This can prevent overeating and make it easier to maintain a healthy weight.

In addition to portion control and balanced meals, the GOLO Diet emphasizes the importance of mindful eating. This involves paying attention to hunger cues and eating slowly, savoring each bite. Mindful eating can help individuals better recognize when they are full, preventing overeating and contributing to a healthier relationship with food.

In summary, the GOLO Diet is a comprehensive approach to weight loss and healthy living that targets insulin resistance and emphasizes balanced nutrition. By focusing on metabolic fuel, portion control, and mindful eating, the diet helps individuals achieve sustainable weight loss and improve their overall health. As you embark on your journey with the GOLO Diet, this cookbook will provide you with the essential recipes and guidance you need to succeed. With a wide variety of delicious and nutritious meal options, you'll be well on your way to a healthier, happier, and more vibrant life.

Getting Started with the GOLO Diet

Preparing Your Kitchen

Essential kitchen tools and equipment

Before diving into the GOLO Diet, it's essential to ensure your kitchen is well-equipped to support your new eating habits. Having the right tools and equipment on hand can make meal preparation easier and more enjoyable. Here are some essentials to consider:

Measuring cups and spoons: Precise measurements are crucial for portion control and balanced meals.

Food scale: A food scale can help you accurately weigh ingredients, ensuring proper portion sizes.

Sharp knives: A good set of knives will make chopping and slicing ingredients a breeze.

Cutting boards: Invest in a few sturdy cutting boards for different food types (produce, proteins, etc.).

Mixing bowls: A variety of sizes will come in handy for various tasks.

Pots and pans: A selection of high-quality pots and pans, including non-stick options, will make cooking easier.

Baking sheets: These are essential for roasting vegetables, baking proteins, and more.

Blender or food processor: Useful for creating smoothies, sauces, and dressings.

Storage containers: Airtight containers in various sizes are essential for meal prepping and keeping leftovers fresh.

Pantry staples

Having a well-stocked pantry can simplify meal planning and preparation. Here are some pantry staples to consider for the GOLO Diet:

Whole grains: Brown rice, quinoa, barley, whole grain pasta, and whole grain bread.

Legumes: Lentils, chickpeas, black beans, and kidney beans.

Nuts and seeds: Almonds, walnuts, chia seeds, and flaxseeds.

Healthy oils: Olive oil, avocado oil, and coconut oil.

Vinegars: Apple cider vinegar, balsamic vinegar, and red wine vinegar.

Herbs and spices: Keep a variety of dried herbs and spices on hand to add flavor to your meals without added calories.

Canned goods: Low-sodium canned vegetables, tomato sauce, and canned fish (such as tuna or salmon) can be convenient options.

Natural sweeteners: Stevia, honey, and pure maple syrup.

Condiments: Mustard, hot sauce, and low-sodium soy sauce can add flavor to your meals.

Shopping tips for the GOLO Diet

When shopping for the GOLO Diet, keep the following tips in mind:

Shop the perimeter: Focus on fresh produce, lean proteins, and whole grains, which are usually located along the perimeter of the grocery store.

Read labels: Pay attention to ingredient lists and nutrition facts to ensure you're making healthy choices.

Choose organic and grass-fed options when possible: These options often have higher nutrient content and fewer additives.

Buy in-season produce: In-season fruits and vegetables are fresher, tastier, and often more affordable.

Meal Planning and Preparation

Creating a meal plan

Creating a meal plan is an essential step in staying organized and ensuring you have everything you need for the week ahead. Here are some tips for creating a GOLO Diet meal plan:

Start with your protein: Choose a variety of lean proteins, such as chicken, turkey, fish, and plant-based options like tofu or tempeh.

Add vegetables: Incorporate plenty of non-starchy vegetables for added nutrients, fiber, and flavor.

Include healthy fats: Avocado, nuts, seeds, and olive oil are excellent sources of healthy fats.

Balance your carbohydrates: Opt for whole grains and complex carbohydrates for steady energy release.

Plan for leftovers: Make extra portions to have on hand for quick and easy meals throughout the week.

Allocate snacks: Plan for healthy snacks like fresh fruit, nuts, or yogurt to keep hunger at bay between meals.

Consider your schedule: Be realistic about your available time for meal preparation, and choose recipes that fit your lifestyle.

Tips for meal prepping

Meal prepping can be a game-changer when it comes to staying on track with the GOLO Diet. Here are some helpful tips for successful meal prepping:

Dedicate time: Set aside a few hours on a designated day each week to prepare meals in advance.

Cook in bulk: Make large batches of grains, proteins, and vegetables that can be easily repurposed into different meals throughout the week.

Use your freezer: Freeze pre-portioned meals or ingredients for quick and easy meals on busy days.

Prepare grab-and-go options: Pre-portion snacks and store them in accessible containers for easy snacking throughout the week.

Keep it simple: Stick to recipes with minimal ingredients and straightforward preparation to save time and reduce stress.

Adapting recipes for dietary restrictions

The GOLO Diet is designed to be adaptable to various dietary preferences and requirements. If you have specific dietary restrictions, consider the following tips for modifying recipes:

For vegetarian or vegan diets: Replace animal proteins with plant-based options like tofu, tempeh, or legumes. Use plant-based milk alternatives and dairy-free cheese substitutes as needed.

For gluten-free diets: Choose gluten-free grains like quinoa, rice, or certified gluten-free oats. Replace wheat flour with gluten-free alternatives like almond flour or rice flour.

For dairy-free diets: Use plant-based milk alternatives, such as almond or coconut milk, and choose dairy-free cheese and yogurt substitutes.

For nut allergies: Replace nuts with seeds (e.g., sunflower or pumpkin seeds) or other crunchy alternatives like roasted chickpeas.

For low-sodium diets: Reduce or eliminate added salt in recipes and use herbs, spices, and vinegar for flavor instead. Opt for low-sodium versions of canned goods and condiments.

By implementing these tips and strategies, you'll be well-prepared to embark on your journey with the GOLO Diet. As you follow this guide and explore the recipes in this cookbook, you'll discover how enjoyable and satisfying healthy eating can be. Embrace the journey and enjoy the process of transforming your health and well-being through the power of balanced nutrition.

Breakfast

Green Smoothie

Ingredients:

- 1 cup spinach leaves
- 1/2 cup sliced cucumber
- 1/2 cup sliced kiwi
- 1/2 banana
- 1/2 cup unsweetened almond milk
- 1 tablespoon chia seeds
- Ice cubes (optional)

Instructions:

1. Wash the spinach leaves and cucumber, and slice the kiwi and banana.
2. In a blender, combine the spinach leaves, sliced cucumber, sliced kiwi, banana, unsweetened almond milk, and chia seeds.
3. Blend the ingredients together until smooth, adding ice cubes if desired for a thicker texture.
4. Pour the green smoothie into a glass and serve immediately, garnished with extra chia seeds or sliced kiwi if desired.

Berry Protein Shake

Ingredients:

- 1/2 cup mixed berries
- 1 scoop vanilla protein powder
- 1/2 cup unsweetened almond milk
- 1/2 cup water
- 1 tablespoon chia seeds
- Ice cubes (optional)

Instructions

1. Wash the mixed berries and add them to a blender.
2. Add the vanilla protein powder, unsweetened almond milk, water, and chia seeds to the blender.
3. Blend the ingredients together until smooth, adding ice cubes if desired for a thicker texture.
4. Pour the berry protein shake into a glass and serve immediately, garnished with extra mixed berries or chia seeds if desired.

Veggie Omelette

Ingredients:

- 2 eggs
- 1/4 cup sliced bell peppers
- 1/4 cup sliced mushrooms
- 1/4 cup diced onions
- 1/4 cup baby spinach leaves
- 1/4 cup shredded low-fat cheese
- Salt and pepper, to taste
- 1 teaspoon olive oil

Instructions:

1. In a bowl, whisk together the eggs with salt and pepper to taste.

2. Heat the olive oil in a non-stick skillet over medium heat.

3. Add the sliced bell peppers, mushrooms, and onions to the skillet and sauté for 3-4 minutes, or until the vegetables are softened.

4. Add the baby spinach leaves to the skillet and sauté for an additional minute, until the spinach is wilted.

5. Pour the whisked eggs over the vegetables in the skillet, and use a spatula to spread the eggs evenly across the skillet

6. Sprinkle the shredded low-fat cheese over the top of the omelette.

Breakfast

7. Cook the omelette for 3-4 minutes, or until the eggs are set and the cheese is melted.

8. Use a spatula to fold the omelette in half, and slide it onto a plate.

9. Serve the veggie omelette immediately, garnished with additional salt and pepper if desired.

Egg Muffins

Ingredients:

- 2 eggs
- 1/4 cup chopped vegetables
- 1/4 cup shredded low-fat cheese
- Salt and pepper, to taste
- Cooking spray

Instructions:

1. Preheat the oven to 350°F (175°C).
2. In a bowl, whisk together the eggs with salt and pepper to taste.
3. Add the chopped vegetables to the bowl and stir to combine.
4. Grease a muffin tin with cooking spray.
5. Divide the egg and vegetable mixture evenly between the muffin cups.
6. Sprinkle the shredded low-fat cheese over the top of each egg muffin.
7. Bake the egg muffins for 15-20 minutes, or until the eggs are set and the cheese is melted and lightly browned.
8. Remove the egg muffins from the oven and allow them to cool for a few minutes.
9. Use a spoon or spatula to gently remove the egg muffins from the muffin tin.
10. Serve the egg muffins immediately, garnished with additional chopped vegetables or herbs if desired.

Breakfast

Healthy and low-calorie egg muffins packed with protein, veggies, and low-fat cheese are a great option for the Golo Diet. Make them ahead of time and store in the fridge for an easy and nutritious meal or snack.

Chia Seed Pudding

Ingredients:

- 1/4 cup chia seeds

- 1 cup unsweetened almond milk

- 1/4 teaspoon vanilla extract

- 1 tablespoon honey or maple syrup

- Mixed berries or sliced fruit, for topping

Instructions:

1. In a bowl, whisk together the chia seeds, unsweetened almond milk, vanilla extract, and honey or maple syrup

2. Cover the bowl with plastic wrap and refrigerate for at least 2 hours or overnight, until the chia seeds have absorbed the liquid and the mixture has thickened.

3. Stir the chia seed pudding well before serving.

4. Spoon the chia seed pudding into a bowl or glass, and top with mixed berries or sliced fruit.

5. Serve the chia seed pudding immediately, garnished with additional honey or maple syrup if desired.

This chia seed pudding recipe is a delicious and healthy dessert or snack option that is perfect for the Golo Diet. Chia seeds are a good source of fiber, protein, and healthy fats, while unsweetened almond milk is low in calories and a good source of calcium and vitamin E. This recipe can be customized with your favorite fruits and toppings, and is a convenient make-ahead option that can be stored in the refrigerator for several days.

Breakfast

Greek Yogurt Parfait

Ingredients

- 1/2 cup plain Greek yogurt
- 1/4 cup mixed berries
- 1/4 cup chopped nuts
- 1/4 teaspoon vanilla extract
- 1 tablespoon honey or maple syrup

Instructions:

1. In a bowl, stir together the plain Greek yogurt, vanilla extract, and honey or maple syrup.
2. Spoon half of the Greek yogurt mixture into a glass or jar.
3. Layer half of the mixed berries and chopped nuts on top of the Greek yogurt.
4. Spoon the remaining Greek yogurt mixture over the top of the berries and nuts.
5. Layer the remaining mixed berries and chopped nuts over the top of the Greek yogurt.
6. Serve the Greek yogurt parfait immediately, garnished with additional berries and nuts if desired.

This Greek yogurt parfait recipe is a nutritious and delicious breakfast or snack option that is perfect for the Golo Diet. Greek yogurt is a good source of protein and calcium, while mixed berries and nuts provide fiber, vitamins, and healthy fats. This recipe can be customized with your favorite fruits and toppings, and is a convenient make-ahead option that can be stored in the refrigerator for several days.

Breakfast Quinoa Bowl

Ingredients:

- 1/4 cup quinoa
- 1/2 cup unsweetened almond milk
- 1/4 cup mixed berries
- 1/4 cup chopped nuts
- 1/4 teaspoon cinnamon
- 1 tablespoon honey or maple syrup

Instructions:

1. Rinse the quinoa in a fine mesh strainer and place it in a small saucepan with the unsweetened almond milk.
2. Bring the quinoa and almond milk to a boil over medium-high heat.
3. Reduce the heat to low, cover the saucepan, and simmer the quinoa for 15-20 minutes, or until all of the liquid has been absorbed and the quinoa is cooked through.
4. Fluff the cooked quinoa with a fork and stir in the cinnamon and honey or maple syrup.
5. Spoon the cooked quinoa into a bowl.
6. Top the quinoa with mixed berries and chopped nuts.
7. Serve the breakfast quinoa bowl immediately, garnished with additional honey or maple syrup if desired.

This breakfast quinoa bowl recipe is a nutritious and filling meal for the Golo Diet. It includes quinoa, almond milk, mixed berries, and nuts, providing protein, fiber, healthy fats, calcium, and vitamins. It's customizable with your preferred toppings, and can be made ahead and stored in the fridge for several days.

Spinach and Mushroom Frittata

Ingredients:

- 2 eggs
- 1/4 cup sliced mushrooms
- 1/4 cup baby spinach leaves
- 1/4 cup diced onions
- 1/4 cup shredded low-fat cheese
- Salt and pepper, to taste
- 1 teaspoon olive oil

Instructions:

1. Preheat the oven to 350°F (175°C).
2. In a bowl, whisk together the eggs with salt and pepper to taste.
3. Heat the olive oil in a small oven-safe skillet over medium heat.
4. Add the sliced mushrooms and diced onions to the skillet and sauté for 3-4 minutes, or until the vegetables are softened.
5. Add the baby spinach leaves to the skillet and sauté for an additional minute, until the spinach is wilted.
6. Pour the whisked eggs over the vegetables in the skillet, and use a spatula to spread the eggs evenly across the skillet.
7. Sprinkle the shredded low-fat cheese over the top of the frittata.

8. Cook the frittata on the stove for 2-3 minutes, or until the edges are set.

9. Transfer the skillet to the oven and bake the frittata for 10-12 minutes, or until the eggs are set and the cheese is melted and lightly browned.

10. Serve the spinach and mushroom frittata immediately, garnished with additional salt and pepper if desired.

This spinach and mushroom frittata is a tasty and nutritious breakfast or brunch option for the Golo Diet. It's high in protein, healthy fats, and fiber, and low in calories. You can customize it with your preferred veggies and spices for added flavor.

Almond Flour Pancakes

Ingredients:

- 1/4 cup almond flour
- 1/4 teaspoon baking powder
- 1/4 teaspoon cinnamon
- 1 egg
- 1/4 cup unsweetened almond milk
- 1/4 teaspoon vanilla extract
- Cooking spray

Instructions:

1. In a bowl, whisk together the almond flour, baking powder, and cinnamon.
2. Add the egg, unsweetened almond milk, and vanilla extract to the bowl and whisk together until smooth.
3. Heat a non-stick skillet over medium heat.
4. Spray the skillet with cooking spray.
5. Pour the batter into the skillet, using a 1/4 cup measure to make small pancakes.
6. Cook the pancakes for 2-3 minutes on each side, or until they are golden brown and cooked through.
7. Serve the almond flour pancakes immediately, garnished with mixed berries or sliced

fruit and a drizzle of honey or maple syrup if desired.

This almond flour pancake recipe is a healthy and delicious breakfast or brunch option for the Golo Diet. It includes almond flour, cinnamon, egg, and unsweetened almond milk, providing protein, healthy fats, calcium, and blood sugar regulation. Customize with your preferred toppings and store in the fridge or freezer for convenience.

Coconut Flour Waffles

Ingredients:

- 1/4 cup coconut flour
- 1/4 teaspoon baking powder
- 1/4 teaspoon cinnamon
- 1 egg
- 1/4 cup unsweetened almond milk
- 1/4 teaspoon vanilla extract
- Cooking spray

Instructions:

1. In a bowl, whisk together the coconut flour, baking powder, and cinnamon.
2. Add the egg, unsweetened almond milk, and vanilla extract to the bowl and whisk together until smooth.
3. Heat a waffle iron and spray with cooking spray.
4. Pour the batter into the waffle iron, using the manufacturer's instructions for cooking time.
5. Serve the coconut flour waffles immediately, garnished with mixed berries or sliced fruit and a drizzle of honey or maple syrup if desired.

This coconut flour waffle recipe is a healthy and tasty breakfast or brunch option for the Golo Diet. It includes coconut flour, cinnamon, egg, and unsweetened almond milk, providing fiber, healthy fats, protein, calcium, and blood sugar regulation. Customize with your preferred toppings and store in the fridge or freezer for convenience.

Savory Oatmeal

Ingredients:

- 1/2 cup rolled oats

- 1 cup low-sodium chicken or vegetable

- 1/4 cup diced onion

- 1/4 cup sliced mushrooms

- 1/4 cup baby spinach leaves

- 1/4 teaspoon garlic powder

- Salt and pepper, to taste

- 1 teaspoon olive oil

- 1 tablespoon shredded low-fat cheese

Instructions:

1. In a small saucepan, bring the low-sodium chicken or vegetable broth to a boil over high heat.

2. Add the rolled oats to the saucepan and reduce the heat to low.

3. Cover the saucepan and simmer the oats for 5-7 minutes, or until they are cooked through and the liquid has been absorbed.

4. While the oats are cooking, heat the olive oil in a small skillet over medium heat.

5. Add the diced onion and sliced mushrooms to the skillet and sauté for 3-4 minutes, or until the vegetables are softened.

Breakfast

6. Add the baby spinach leaves to the skillet and sauté for an additional minute, until the spinach is wilted.

7. Stir the garlic powder, salt, and pepper into the cooked oats.

8. Spoon the cooked oats into a bowl.

9. Top the oats with the sautéed vegetables.

10. Sprinkle the shredded low-fat cheese over the top of the oatmeal

11. Serve the savory oatmeal immediately, garnished with additional salt and pepper if desired.

This savory oatmeal recipe is a nutritious and satisfying meal for the Golo Diet. Rolled oats provide fiber and protein, while low-sodium broth adds flavor and nutrients. Sautéed vegetables add vitamins and minerals, and low-fat cheese adds creaminess. Customize with your preferred veggies and seasonings, and store in the fridge for convenience.

Shakshuka

Ingredients:

- 1 tablespoon olive oil
- 1/4 cup diced onion
- 1/4 cup diced red bell pepper
- 1/4 cup diced zucchini
- 1/4 teaspoon cumin
- 1/4 teaspoon paprika
- 1/8 teaspoon cayenne pepper
- Salt and pepper, to taste
- 1/2 cup canned diced tomatoes
- 1 egg
- 1 tablespoon chopped fresh parsley

Instructions:

1. Heat the olive oil in a small skillet over medium heat.
2. Add the diced onion, red bell pepper, and zucchini to the skillet and sauté for 3-4 minutes, or until the vegetables are softened.
3. Stir in the cumin, paprika, cayenne pepper, salt, and pepper.
4. Add the canned diced tomatoes to the skillet and bring the mixture to a simmer.

Breakfast

5. Use a spoon to make a small well in the tomato mixture.

6. Crack the egg into the well.

7. Cover the skillet and simmer for 5-7 minutes, or until the egg is cooked to your liking.

8. Sprinkle the chopped fresh parsley over the top of the shakshuka (if using).

9. Serve the shakshuka immediately, garnished with additional salt and pepper if desired.

This shakshuka recipe is a tasty and healthy meal for the Golo Diet. Vegetables and spices provide vitamins and minerals, while eggs offer protein and healthy fats. Customize with your preferred veggies and spices and cook in one pan for convenience.

Overnight Oats

Ingredients:

- 1/2 cup rolled oats

- 1/2 cup unsweetened almond milk

- 1/4 cup mixed berries

- 1 tablespoon chia seeds

- 1/4 teaspoon vanilla extract

- 1 tablespoon honey or maple syrup

Instructions:

1. In a jar or bowl, combine the rolled oats, unsweetened almond milk, mixed berries, chia seeds, vanilla extract, and honey or maple syrup (if using).

2. Stir the ingredients together until well combined.

3. Cover the jar or bowl and refrigerate overnight, or for at least 4 hours.

4. Serve the overnight oats chilled, garnished with additional mixed berries and a drizzle of honey or maple syrup if desired.

This overnight oat recipe is a nutritious and convenient breakfast option that is perfect for the Golo Diet. Rolled oats are a good source of fiber and protein, while unsweetened almond milk provides additional calcium and vitamin E. Mixed berries add vitamins and antioxidants, while chia seeds provide healthy omega-3 fatty acids. This recipe can be customized with your favorite fruits and toppings, and is a perfect make-ahead option that can be stored in the refrigerator for several days.

Sweet Potato Hash

Ingredients:

- 1 small sweet potato, peeled and diced
- 1/4 cup diced onion
- 1/4 cup diced red bell pepper
- 1/4 cup sliced mushrooms
- 1/4 teaspoon garlic powder
- Salt and pepper, to taste
- 1 tablespoon olive oil
- 1 egg
- 1 tablespoon chopped fresh parsley

Instructions:

1. Heat the olive oil in a small skillet over medium heat.
2. Add the diced sweet potato, onion, and red bell pepper to the skillet and sauté for 5-7 minutes, or until the sweet potato is softened.
3. Stir in the sliced mushrooms, garlic powder, salt, and pepper.
4. Continue to cook the sweet potato hash for an additional 3-4 minutes, or until the mushrooms are tender and the sweet potato is golden brown.
5. Use a spoon to make a small well in the sweet potato hash.

6. Crack the egg into the well.

7. Cover the skillet and cook for 3-4 minutes, or until the egg is cooked to your liking.

8. Sprinkle the chopped fresh parsley over the top of the sweet potato hash .

9. Serve the sweet potato hash immediately, garnished with additional salt and pepper if desired.

This sweet potato hash recipe is a nutritious and flavorful meal for the Golo Diet. Sweet potato provides fiber and vitamins, while veggies and spices add more nutrients. Eggs offer protein and healthy fats. Customize with your preferred veggies and seasonings and cook in one pan for convenience.

Broccoli and Cheese Egg Cups

Ingredients:

- 2 eggs
- 1/4 cup diced broccoli florets
- 1 tablespoon diced red bell pepper
- 1 tablespoon diced onion
- 1/4 cup shredded low-fat cheese
- Salt and pepper, to taste
- Cooking spray

Instructions:

1. Preheat the oven to 350°F (175°C).
2. Spray a muffin tin with cooking spray.
3. In a bowl, whisk together the eggs, diced broccoli florets, diced red bell pepper, diced onion, shredded low-fat cheese, salt, and pepper.
4. Pour the egg mixture into the prepared muffin tin, filling each cup about 2/3 full.
5. Bake the egg cups for 15-20 minutes, or until they are set and golden brown on top.
6. Remove the egg cups from the oven and let them cool for a few minutes.
7. Use a spoon or knife to loosen the egg cups from the muffin tin.

8. Serve the broccoli and cheese egg cups immediately, garnished with additional salt and pepper if desired.

This broccoli and cheese egg cup recipe is a tasty and healthy breakfast or snack for the Golo Diet. Eggs provide protein and healthy fats, while broccoli adds vitamins and . Diced pepper and onion add flavor and nutrients, and low-fat cheese adds creaminess. Store in the fridge for several days as a convenient make-ahead option.

Breakfast

Banana Almond Smoothie

Ingredients:

- 1 medium ripe banana
- 1/2 cup unsweetened almond milk
- 1/4 cup plain Greek yogurt
- 1/4 cup raw almonds
- 1/4 teaspoon vanilla extract
- 1/2 cup ice cubes

Instructions:

1. Add the ripe banana, unsweetened almond milk, plain Greek yogurt, raw almonds, vanilla extract, and ice cubes to a blender.

2. Blend the ingredients together until smooth and creamy.

3. Pour the banana almond smoothie into a glass.

4. Serve the smoothie immediately, garnished with additional raw almonds or sliced banana if desired.

This banana almond smoothie recipe is a nutritious and delicious breakfast or snack option that is perfect for the Golo Diet. Bananas provide fiber and natural sweetness, while unsweetened almond milk and Greek yogurt provide protein and calcium. Raw almonds add healthy fats and crunch, while vanilla extract provides a hint of sweetness. This recipe can be customized with your favorite fruits and nuts, and is a perfect on-the-go option that can be prepared in minutes.

Granola and Yogurt Bowl

Ingredients:

- 1/2 cup plain Greek yogurt
- 1/4 cup mixed berries
- 1/4 cup granola
- 1 tablespoon raw honey or maple

Instructions:

1. Spoon the plain Greek yogurt into a bowl.
2. Top the yogurt with the mixed berries.
3. Sprinkle the granola over the top of the berries and yogurt.
4. Drizzle the raw honey or maple syrup over the top of the granola (if using).
5. Serve the granola and yogurt bowl immediately, garnished with additional mixed berries and a drizzle of honey or maple syrup if desired.

This granola and yogurt bowl recipe is a nutritious and satisfying breakfast or snack option that is perfect for the Golo Diet. Greek yogurt provides protein and calcium, while mixed berries add vitamins and antioxidants. The addition of granola provides fiber and crunch, making this bowl a balanced and delicious meal. This recipe can be customized with your favorite fruits and nuts, and is a perfect make-ahead option that can be stored in the refrigerator for several days.

Vegetable Scramble

Ingredients:

- 2 eggs
- 1/4 cup diced zucchini
- 1/4 cup diced red bell pepper
- 1/4 cup sliced mushrooms
- 1/4 cup diced onion
- Salt and pepper, to taste
- 1 tablespoon olive oil
- 1/2 small avocado, diced

Instructions:

1. In a bowl, whisk together the eggs and salt and pepper to taste.
2. Heat the olive oil in a small skillet over medium heat.
3. Add the diced zucchini, red bell pepper, sliced mushrooms, and diced onion to the skillet and sauté for 3-4 minutes, or until the vegetables are softened.
4. Pour the whisked eggs into the skillet with the vegetables.
5. Stir the mixture continuously until the eggs are scrambled and cooked to your liking.
6. Transfer the vegetable scramble to a plate.
7. Serve the vegetable scramble immediately, garnished with diced avocado (if using).

This vegetable scramble recipe is a nutritious and satisfying breakfast or brunch for the Golo Diet. Eggs offer protein and healthy fats, while veggies provide vitamins and minerals. Customize with your preferred veggies and spices, and cook in one pan for convenience. Diced avocado adds healthy fats and creaminess to make it even more satisfying.

Breakfast

Baked Oatmeal

Ingredients:

- 1/2 cup rolled oats
- 1/4 teaspoon cinnamon
- 1/4 teaspoon baking powder
- 1/4 teaspoon vanilla extract
- 1 tablespoon honey or maple syrup
- 1/2 cup unsweetened almond milk
- 1 egg
- 1/4 cup mixed berries
- Cooking spray

Instructions:

1. Preheat the oven to 375°F (190°C).
2. Spray a small baking dish with cooking spray.
3. In a bowl, combine the rolled oats, cinnamon, baking powder, vanilla extract, and honey or maple syrup.
4. In a separate bowl, whisk together the unsweetened almond milk and egg.
5. Add the wet ingredients to the dry ingredients and stir until well combined.
6. Fold in the mixed berries.

7. Pour the oatmeal mixture into the prepared baking dish.

8. Bake the oatmeal for 20-25 minutes, or until the top is golden brown and the oatmeal is set.

9. Remove the oatmeal from the oven and let it cool for a few minutes.

10. Serve the baked oatmeal warm, garnished with additional mixed berries if desired.

This baked oatmeal recipe is a nutritious and tasty breakfast or brunch for the Golo Diet. Rolled oats provide fiber and protein, while cinnamon, vanilla extract, and mixed berries add flavor and nutrients. Customize with your preferred fruits and nuts, and store in the fridge for several days. Almond milk and egg provide protein and healthy fats, making it a balanced and satisfying meal.

Breakfast

Quinoa Breakfast Porridge

Ingredients:

- 1/2 cup cooked quinoa

- 1/2 cup unsweetened almond milk

- 1/2 cup mixed berries

- 1 tablespoon chopped raw almonds

- 1/4 teaspoon vanilla extract

- 1 tablespoon raw honey or maple syrup

Instructions:

1. In a small saucepan, combine the cooked quinoa and unsweetened almond milk.

2. Cook the quinoa and almond milk over medium heat, stirring frequently, for 3-4 minutes or until the mixture is heated through and creamy.

3. Stir in the mixed berries, chopped raw almonds, vanilla extract, and raw honey or maple syrup (if using).

4. Continue to cook the quinoa breakfast porridge for an additional 1-2 minutes, or until the berries are heated through and the almonds are slightly toasted.

5. Serve the quinoa breakfast porridge immediately, garnished with additional mixed berries and chopped almonds if desired.

This quinoa breakfast porridge recipe is a nutritious and flavorful meal for the Golo Diet. Cooked quinoa provides protein and fiber, while almond milk adds calcium and creaminess. Mixed berries and raw almonds offer vitamins, minerals, and healthy fats, making it a balanced and delicious meal. Customize with your preferred fruits and nuts and store in the fridge for several days as a convenient make-ahead option.

Lunch

Greek Salad with Chicken

Ingredients:

- 2 cups mixed greens
- 1/2 cup sliced cucumber
- 1/4 cup sliced red onion
- 1/4 cup sliced cherry tomatoes
- 1/4 cup crumbled feta cheese
- 1/2 grilled chicken breast, sliced
- 1 tablespoon extra-virgin olive oil
- 1 tablespoon red wine vinegar
- Salt and pepper, to taste

Instructions:

1. In a large bowl, combine the mixed greens, sliced cucumber, sliced red onion, and sliced cherry tomatoes.
2. Top the salad with the crumbled feta cheese and sliced grilled chicken breast.
3. Drizzle the extra-virgin olive oil and red wine vinegar over the top of the salad.
4. Season the salad with salt and pepper to taste.
5. Toss the salad gently until the ingredients are well combined.
6. Serve the Greek salad with chicken immediately.

Lunch

This Greek salad with chicken recipe is a nutritious and satisfying lunch or dinner option that is perfect for the Golo Diet. Mixed greens provide fiber and vitamins, while sliced cucumber and cherry tomatoes add hydration and nutrients. Grilled chicken breast provides protein, while crumbled feta cheese adds flavor and healthy fats. The addition of extra-virgin olive oil and red wine vinegar provide a tangy and flavorful dressing that complements the ingredients perfectly. This recipe can be customized with your favorite vegetables and toppings, and is a perfect meal option for busy weekdays or on-the-go lunches.

Tuna Salad Lettuce Wraps

Ingredients:

- 1 can (4 oz) of tuna in water, drained
- 1 tablespoon diced red onion
- 1 tablespoon diced celery
- 1 tablespoon chopped fresh parsley
- 1 tablespoon lemon juice
- Salt and pepper, to taste
- 2 large lettuce leaves
- 1/4 avocado, sliced
- 1/4 cup sliced cherry tomatoes

Instructions:

1. In a bowl, combine the drained tuna, diced red onion, diced celery, chopped fresh parsley, and lemon juice.
2. Season the tuna salad with salt and pepper to taste.
3. Arrange the large lettuce leaves on a plate.
4. Divide the tuna salad mixture between the two lettuce leaves.
5. Top the tuna salad with sliced avocado and sliced cherry tomatoes.
6. Serve the tuna salad lettuce wraps immediately.

Lunch

This tuna salad lettuce wraps recipe is a nutritious and flavorful meal for the Golo Diet. Tuna offers protein and healthy fats, while red onion, celery, parsley, and lemon juice add flavor. Lettuce leaves replace traditional wraps, making it low-carb. Avocado and cherry tomatoes provide healthy fats, vitamins, and antioxidants. Customize with your preferred veggies and herbs, and it's a perfect on-the-go meal.

Cauliflower Fried Rice

Ingredients:

- 1 cup riced cauliflower
- 1/4 cup diced onion
- 1/4 cup diced red bell pepper
- 1/4 cup diced carrots
- 1/4 cup frozen peas
- 1 egg
- 1 tablespoon low-sodium soy sauce
- 1 tablespoon olive oil
- Salt and pepper, to taste

Instructions:

1. In a small skillet, heat the olive oil over medium heat.
2. Add the diced onion, red bell pepper, and carrots to the skillet and sauté for 3-4 minutes, or until the vegetables are softened.
3. Add the riced cauliflower and frozen peas to the skillet and sauté for an additional 3-4 minutes, or until the cauliflower is heated through and slightly softened.
4. Push the vegetables to one side of the skillet and crack the egg into the empty side of the skillet.
5. Scramble the egg with a spatula until cooked, and then stir it into the vegetable mixture.

Lunch

6. Drizzle the low-sodium soy sauce over the top of the cauliflower fried rice.

7. Season the cauliflower fried rice with salt and pepper to taste.

8. Serve the cauliflower fried rice immediately.

This cauliflower fried rice recipe is a nutritious and flavorful meal for the Golo Diet. Riced cauliflower replaces traditional rice, making it low-carb. Onion, red bell pepper, carrots, and peas provide flavor and nutrients, while scrambled egg adds protein and healthy fats. Low-sodium soy sauce adds a savory taste. Customize with your preferred veggies and protein sources, and it's great for meal prep or busy weekdays.

Turkey and Avocado Sandwich

Ingredients:

- 2 slices of whole grain bread
- 2-3 oz of sliced turkey breast
- 1/4 avocado, mashed
- 1/4 cup sliced cucumber
- 1/4 cup sliced cherry tomatoes
- 1/4 cup mixed greens
- 1 tablespoon Dijon mustard
- Salt and pepper, to taste

Instructions:

1. Toast the slices of whole grain bread until lightly browned.
2. Spread the mashed avocado on one slice of the toasted bread.
3. Layer the sliced turkey breast on top of the mashed avocado.
4. Top the turkey with sliced cucumber, cherry tomatoes, and mixed greens.
5. Spread the Dijon mustard on the other slice of toasted bread.
6. Season the sandwich with salt and pepper to taste.
7. Place the Dijon mustard slice of bread on top of the other slice, pressing gently to form a sandwich.
8. Cut the sandwich in half and serve immediately.

Lunch

This turkey and avocado sandwich recipe is a nutritious and satisfying lunch for the Golo Diet. Whole grain bread provides fiber and complex carbs, while turkey breast adds protein. Mashed avocado offers healthy fats and creaminess, while cucumber, tomatoes, and mixed greens provide hydration and nutrients. Dijon mustard adds a tangy flavor. Customize with your preferred veggies and protein sources, and it's great for meal prep or on-the-go lunches.

Zucchini Noodle Salad

Ingredients:

- 1 medium zucchini, spiralized into noodles
- 1/4 cup sliced cherry tomatoes
- 1/4 cup diced red onion
- 1/4 cup sliced black olives
- 1/4 cup crumbled feta cheese
- 2 tablespoons extra-virgin olive oil
- 1 tablespoon red wine vinegar
- 1 clove garlic, minced
- Salt and pepper, to taste

Instructions:

1. In a large bowl, combine the zucchini noodles, sliced cherry tomatoes, diced red onion, and sliced black olives.
2. Top the salad with the crumbled feta cheese.
3. In a small bowl, whisk together the extra-virgin olive oil, red wine vinegar, minced garlic, salt, and pepper.
4. Drizzle the dressing over the top of the zucchini noodle salad.
5. Toss the salad gently until the ingredients are well combined and coated in the dressing.

Lunch

6. Serve the zucchini noodle salad immediately.

This zucchini noodle salad recipe is a nutritious and flavorful meal for the Golo Diet. Zucchini noodles replace traditional pasta, making it low-carb. Cherry tomatoes, red onion, black olives, and feta cheese provide flavor and healthy fats. Olive oil, red wine vinegar, and garlic create a tangy dressing. Customize with your preferred veggies and toppings, and store in the fridge for several days as a convenient make-ahead option.

Grilled Veggie Quinoa Bowl

Ingredients:

- 1/2 cup cooked quinoa
- 1/4 cup sliced red onion
- 1/4 cup sliced zucchini
- 1/4 cup sliced yellow squash
- 1/4 cup sliced bell peppers
- 1/4 cup sliced mushrooms
- 1 tablespoon extra-virgin olive oil
- 1 tablespoon balsamic vinegar
- 1 clove garlic, minced
- Salt and pepper, to taste

Instructions:

1. Preheat a grill or grill pan over medium-high heat.
2. In a large bowl, toss the sliced red onion, zucchini, yellow squash, bell peppers, and mushrooms with the extra-virgin olive oil, balsamic vinegar, minced garlic, salt, and pepper.
3. Grill the vegetables for 5-7 minutes, or until they are charred and softened.
4. In a serving bowl, arrange the cooked quinoa in the bottom.
5. Top the quinoa with the grilled vegetables.

Lunch

6. Drizzle any remaining dressing from the bowl over the top of the quinoa bowl.

7. Serve the grilled veggie quinoa bowl immediately.

This grilled veggie quinoa bowl recipe is a nutritious and flavorful meal for the Golo Diet. Quinoa provides protein and complex carbs, while grilled veggies add flavor and nutrients. Customize with your preferred grilled veggies and toppings. Olive oil, balsamic vinegar, garlic, salt, and pepper make a tangy dressing. Perfect for meal prep and can be stored in the fridge for several days.

Shrimp and Asparagus Stir-Fry

Ingredients:

- 4 oz raw shrimp, peeled and deveined
- 1/2 cup chopped asparagus
- 1/4 cup sliced red bell pepper
- 1/4 cup sliced yellow onion
- 1 clove garlic, minced
- 1 tablespoon coconut oil
- 1 tablespoon low-sodium soy sauce
- 1 teaspoon honey
- Salt and pepper, to taste

Instructions:

1. In a small bowl, whisk together the low-sodium soy sauce and honey.

2. In a large skillet or wok, heat the coconut oil over medium-high heat.

3. Add the chopped asparagus, sliced red bell pepper, and sliced yellow onion to the skillet and stir-fry for 3-4 minutes, or until the vegetables are slightly softened.

4. Add the minced garlic to the skillet and stir-fry for an additional 30 seconds, or until fragrant.

5. Add the peeled and deveined raw shrimp to the skillet and stir-fry for 2-3 minutes, or until the shrimp are pink and cooked through.

Lunch

6. Pour the soy sauce and honey mixture over the shrimp and vegetable mixture.

7. Stir the mixture until the ingredients are well coated in the sauce.

8. Season the shrimp and asparagus stir-fry with salt and pepper to taste.

9. Serve the shrimp and asparagus stir-fry immediately.

This shrimp and asparagus stir-fry recipe is a nutritious and flavorful meal for the Golo Diet. Shrimp offers lean protein, while asparagus, red bell pepper, and onion provide flavor and nutrients. Garlic adds a savory taste. Soy sauce and honey dress the shrimp and veggies, adding a sweet and tangy flavor. Customize with your preferred veggies and protein sources. Great for meal prep or busy weekdays.

Chicken Fajita Salad

Ingredients:

- 4 oz grilled chicken breast, sliced
- 1/2 cup sliced bell peppers
- 1/4 cup sliced red onion
- 1/4 cup sliced cherry tomatoes
- 1/4 avocado, sliced
- 2 cups mixed greens
- 1 tablespoon extra-virgin olive oil
- 1 tablespoon lime juice
- 1/2 teaspoon chili powder
- 1/2 teaspoon ground cumin
- Salt and pepper, to taste

Instructions:

1. In a small bowl, whisk together the extra-virgin olive oil, lime juice, chili powder, ground cumin, salt, and pepper.
2. In a large bowl, combine the sliced grilled chicken breast, sliced bell peppers, sliced red onion, sliced cherry tomatoes, sliced avocado, and mixed greens.
3. Pour the dressing over the top of the salad.
4. Toss the salad gently until the ingredients are well combined and coated in the dressing.

Lunch

5. Serve the chicken fajita salad immediately.

This chicken fajita salad recipe is a nutritious and flavorful meal for the Golo Diet. Grilled chicken breast provides lean protein, while bell peppers, red onion, cherry tomatoes, and avocado add flavor and nutrients. Mixed greens offer vitamins and minerals. Olive oil, lime juice, chili powder, cumin, salt, and pepper create a tangy dressing. Customize with your preferred veggies and protein sources, and store in the fridge for several days as a make-ahead option.

Spinach and Quinoa Stuffed Peppers

Ingredients:

- 1 medium bell pepper, halved and seeded
- 1/4 cup cooked quinoa
- 1/4 cup chopped spinach
- 1/4 cup chopped tomato
- 1/4 cup diced red onion
- 1/4 cup crumbled feta cheese
- 1 tablespoon extra-virgin olive oil
- 1 clove garlic, minced
- Salt and pepper, to taste

Instructions:

1. Preheat the oven to 375°F (190°C).
2. In a small bowl, combine the cooked quinoa, chopped spinach, chopped tomato, diced red onion, crumbled feta cheese, extra-virgin olive oil, minced garlic, salt, and pepper.
3. Stuff the mixture into the halved bell pepper.
4. Place the stuffed bell pepper halves on a baking sheet.
5. Bake the stuffed peppers in the oven for 25-30 minutes, or until the pepper is tender and the filling is heated through.

Lunch

6. Serve the spinach and quinoa stuffed peppers immediately.

This spinach and quinoa stuffed peppers recipe is a nutritious and flavorful meal for the Golo Diet. Bell peppers provide a low-carb and nutrient-dense base, while quinoa, spinach, tomato, red onion, and feta cheese offer flavor and nutrients. Season with olive oil, garlic, salt, and pepper. Customize with your preferred veggies and toppings, and store in the fridge for several days as a make-ahead option.

Tomato and Mozzarella Salad

Ingredients:

- 1 medium tomato, sliced
- 2 oz fresh mozzarella cheese, sliced
- 1 tablespoon extra-virgin olive oil
- 1 tablespoon balsamic vinegar
- 1 tablespoon chopped fresh basil
- Salt and pepper, to taste

Instructions:

1. On a plate, arrange the sliced tomato and sliced mozzarella cheese.
2. In a small bowl, whisk together the extra-virgin olive oil, balsamic vinegar, chopped fresh basil, salt, and pepper.
3. Drizzle the dressing over the top of the tomato and mozzarella cheese.
4. Serve the tomato and mozzarella salad immediately.

This tomato and mozzarella salad recipe is a simple and flavorful lunch or dinner option that is perfect for the Golo Diet. Sliced tomato provides vitamins and minerals, while fresh mozzarella cheese adds healthy fats and protein. A simple dressing made with extra-virgin olive oil, balsamic vinegar, chopped fresh basil, salt, and pepper provides a tangy and flavorful dressing that complements the ingredients perfectly. This recipe can be customized with your favorite herbs and seasonings, and is a perfect make-ahead option that can be stored in the refrigerator for several hours before serving.

Broccoli and Chicken Stir-Fry

Ingredients:

- 4 oz boneless, skinless chicken breast, sliced
- 1 cup chopped broccoli florets
- 1/2 cup sliced bell peppers
- 1/4 cup sliced red onion
- 1 clove garlic, minced
- 1 tablespoon coconut oil
- 1 tablespoon low-sodium soy sauce
- 1 teaspoon honey
- Salt and pepper, to taste

Instructions:

1. In a small bowl, whisk together the low-sodium soy sauce and honey.
2. In a large skillet or wok, heat the coconut oil over medium-high heat.
3. Add the sliced chicken breast to the skillet and stir-fry for 3-4 minutes, or until the chicken is cooked through.
4. Add the chopped broccoli florets, sliced bell peppers, and sliced red onion to the skillet and stir-fry for 3-4 minutes, or until the vegetables are slightly softened.
5. Add the minced garlic to the skillet and stir-fry for an additional 30 seconds, or until fragrant.

6. Pour the soy sauce and honey mixture over the chicken and vegetable mixture.

7. Stir the mixture until the ingredients are well coated in the sauce.

8. Season the broccoli and chicken stir-fry with salt and pepper to taste.

9. Serve the broccoli and chicken stir-fry immediately.

This chicken and broccoli stir-fry recipe is a nutritious and flavorful option for lunch or dinner on the Golo Diet. Sliced chicken breast and chopped broccoli florets provide protein and nutrients, while sliced bell peppers and red onion add flavor. A simple mixture of soy sauce and honey dresses the dish, making it a sweet and tangy option. This recipe is customizable and can be meal prepped for busy weekdays.

Spaghetti Squash Pad Thai

Ingredients:

- 1 small spaghetti squash
- 1/2 cup cooked, sliced chicken breast
- 1/2 cup sliced bell peppers
- 1/4 cup sliced red onion
- 1/4 cup sliced scallions
- 1/4 cup chopped peanuts
- 1 tablespoon coconut oil
- 1 clove garlic, minced
- 1 tablespoon fish sauce
- 1 tablespoon low-sodium soy sauce
- 1 tablespoon honey
- 1 tablespoon lime juice
- Salt and pepper, to taste

Instructions:

1. Preheat the oven to 375°F (190°C).
2. Cut the spaghetti squash in half lengthwise and remove the seeds.

3. Place the spaghetti squash halves cut-side down on a baking sheet.

4. Roast the spaghetti squash in the oven for 30-40 minutes, or until the flesh is tender and easily comes apart in strands.

5. In a small bowl, whisk together the fish sauce, low-sodium soy sauce, honey, lime juice, minced garlic, salt, and pepper.

6. In a large skillet or wok, heat the coconut oil over medium-high heat.

7. Add the sliced chicken breast to the skillet and stir-fry for 3-4 minutes, or until the chicken is cooked through.

8. Add the sliced bell peppers, sliced red onion, and sliced scallions to the skillet and stir-fry for 2-3 minutes, or until the vegetables are slightly softened.

9. Add the cooked spaghetti squash strands to the skillet and stir-fry for an additional 2-3 minutes, or until the squash is heated through.

10. Pour the fish sauce mixture over the spaghetti squash and vegetable mixture.

11. Stir the mixture until the ingredients are well coated in the sauce.

12. Garnish the spaghetti squash pad Thai with chopped peanuts.

13. Serve the spaghetti squash pad Thai immediately.

Roasted spaghetti squash, sliced chicken, bell peppers, red onion, scallions, and peanuts are dressed with fish sauce, soy sauce, honey, lime juice, garlic, salt, and pepper for a tasty Golo Diet meal. Perfect for meal prep or busy weekdays.

Roasted Vegetable Farro Salad

Ingredients:

- 1/2 cup cooked farro
- 1 cup chopped mixed vegetables
- 1 clove garlic, minced
- 1 tablespoon extra-virgin olive oil
- Salt and pepper, to taste
- 2 cups mixed greens
- 1 tablespoon crumbled feta cheese
- 1 tablespoon chopped fresh herbs
- 1 tablespoon balsamic vinegar
- 1 tablespoon extra-virgin olive oil

Instructions:

1. Preheat the oven to 400°F (200°C).
2. In a large bowl, toss the chopped mixed vegetables with minced garlic, extra-virgin olive oil, salt, and pepper.
3. Spread the vegetable mixture out in a single layer on a baking sheet.
4. Roast the vegetable mixture in the oven for 25-30 minutes, or until the vegetables are tender and slightly caramelized.
5. In a small bowl, whisk together the balsamic vinegar and extra-virgin olive oil.

6. In a serving bowl, combine the cooked farro, mixed greens, crumbled feta cheese, and chopped fresh herbs.

7. Add the roasted vegetable mixture to the serving bowl.

8. Drizzle the balsamic vinegar and extra-virgin olive oil mixture over the salad.

9. Toss the salad until the ingredients are well combined.

10. Season the roasted vegetable farro salad with additional salt and pepper to taste.

11. Serve the roasted vegetable farro salad immediately.

This roasted vegetable farro salad recipe is a nutritious and satisfying lunch or dinner option that is perfect for the Golo Diet. Cooked farro provides fiber and complex carbohydrates, while chopped mixed vegetables provide flavor and nutrients. Roasting the vegetables adds a depth of flavor and caramelization that complements the other ingredients in the dish. Mixed greens provide additional nutrients and freshness, while crumbled feta cheese adds a tangy and creamy element to the dish. A simple dressing made with balsamic vinegar and extra-virgin olive oil adds a sweet and tangy flavor to the salad. This recipe can be customized with your favorite vegetables and herbs, and is a perfect make-ahead option that can be stored in the refrigerator for several hours before serving.

Lentil Soup

Ingredients:

- 1/2 cup dried lentils, rinsed and drained
- 1 cup low-sodium vegetable broth
- 1/2 cup chopped mixed vegetables
- 1 clove garlic, minced
- 1 tablespoon extra-virgin olive oil
- Salt and pepper, to taste
- 1 tablespoon chopped fresh parsley
- 1 tablespoon lemon juice

Instructions:

1. In a small pot, combine the rinsed and drained lentils with the low-sodium vegetable broth.
2. Bring the lentils and broth to a boil over medium-high heat.
3. Reduce the heat to low and simmer the lentils, covered, for 20-25 minutes, or until the lentils are tender.
4. In a separate pan, heat the extra-virgin olive oil over medium-high heat.
5. Add the chopped mixed vegetables to the pan and sauté for 3-4 minutes, or until the vegetables are slightly softened.

6. Add the minced garlic to the pan and sauté for an additional 30 seconds, or until fragrant.

7. Add the sautéed vegetables to the pot with the lentils and broth.

8. Stir the mixture until the ingredients are well combined.

9. Season the lentil soup with salt and pepper to taste.

10. Garnish the lentil soup with chopped fresh parsley and a drizzle of lemon juice.

11. Serve the lentil soup immediately.

This lentil soup recipe is a nutritious and comforting option for the Golo Diet. Dried lentils, mixed vegetables, and garlic are cooked in low-sodium vegetable broth, and garnished with parsley and lemon juice. It's customizable and can be made ahead of time for easy meal planning.

Chicken and Avocado Salad

Ingredients:

- 1/2 cup cooked shredded chicken breast
- 1/2 avocado, diced
- 1/2 cup chopped mixed vegetables
- 1 cup mixed greens
- 1 tablespoon crumbled feta cheese
- 1 tablespoon chopped fresh herbs
- 1 tablespoon extra-virgin olive oil
- 1 tablespoon balsamic vinegar
- Salt and pepper, to taste

Instructions:

1. In a large bowl, combine the cooked shredded chicken breast, diced avocado, and chopped mixed vegetables.
2. Add the mixed greens, crumbled feta cheese, and chopped fresh herbs to the bowl.
3. In a small bowl, whisk together the extra-virgin olive oil and balsamic vinegar.
4. Drizzle the dressing over the salad.
5. Season the chicken and avocado salad with salt and pepper to taste.

6. Toss the salad until the ingredients are well combined.

7. Serve the chicken and avocado salad immediately.

This chicken and avocado salad is a delicious and nutritious meal for the Golo Diet. Cooked shredded chicken, diced avocado, chopped vegetables, mixed greens, crumbled feta cheese, and fresh herbs are dressed with extra-virgin olive oil and balsamic vinegar. This recipe is customizable and perfect for make-ahead meals.

Lunch

Turkey and Veggie Stuffed Pita

Ingredients:

- 1 whole wheat pita
- 1/2 cup cooked ground turkey
- 1/2 cup chopped mixed vegetables
- 1 clove garlic, minced
- 1 tablespoon extra-virgin olive oil
- Salt and pepper, to taste
- 2 tablespoons hummus
- 1/4 cup chopped fresh parsley

Instructions:

1. Preheat the oven to 350°F (175°C).
2. Cut the whole wheat pita in half and gently open the pocket.
3. In a pan, heat the extra-virgin olive oil over medium-high heat.
4. Add the chopped mixed vegetables to the pan and sauté for 3-4 minutes, or until the vegetables are slightly softened.
5. Add the minced garlic to the pan and sauté for an additional 30 seconds, or until fragrant.
6. Add the cooked ground turkey to the pan with the vegetables.
7. Season the turkey and vegetable mixture with salt and pepper to taste.

8. Stuff the pita pocket with the turkey and vegetable mixture.

9. Spread hummus over the top of the stuffed pita.

10. Place the stuffed pita on a baking sheet and bake in the preheated oven for 5-7 minutes, or until the pita is slightly toasted and the filling is warmed through.

11. Garnish the stuffed pita with chopped fresh parsley.

12. Serve the stuffed pita immediately.

This turkey and veggie stuffed pita recipe features ground turkey, mixed vegetables, and hummus in a pita pocket. Sauteed vegetables add flavor, while hummus adds creaminess. This recipe is customizable and can be prepared ahead of time.

Vegetable Chickpea Curry

Ingredients:

- 1/2 cup cooked chickpeas
- 1/2 cup chopped mixed vegetables
- 1/2 cup canned diced tomatoes
- 1/4 cup canned coconut milk
- 1 clove garlic, minced
- 1 tablespoon extra-virgin olive oil
- 1/2 teaspoon ground cumin
- 1/2 teaspoon ground coriander
- 1/2 teaspoon turmeric
- Salt and pepper, to taste
- 1 tablespoon chopped fresh cilantro
- 1/2 cup cooked brown rice

Instructions:

1. In a pan, heat the extra-virgin olive oil over medium-high heat.
2. Add the chopped mixed vegetables to the pan and sauté for 3-4 minutes, or until the vegetables are slightly softened.
3. Add the minced garlic to the pan and sauté for an additional 30 seconds, or until fragrant.

4. Add the ground cumin, ground coriander, and turmeric to the pan with the vegetables.

5. Stir the mixture until the spices are well combined.

6. Add the canned diced tomatoes and cooked chickpeas to the pan.

7. Stir the mixture until the ingredients are well combined.

8. Pour the canned coconut milk over the top of the mixture.

9. Season the chickpea curry with salt and pepper to taste.

10. Simmer the curry over medium heat for 8-10 minutes, or until the vegetables are tender and the flavors are well blended.

11. Garnish the chickpea curry with chopped fresh cilantro.

12. Serve the chickpea curry over a bed of cooked brown rice.

This vegetable chickpea curry is a flavorful and hearty dinner option for the Golo Diet. Chickpeas, mixed vegetables, canned tomatoes, and coconut milk make up the base, while spices and cilantro add flavor and aroma. Serve over cooked brown rice for added fiber and nutrients. This recipe is customizable and can be stored in the refrigerator for several days before reheating.

Cobb Salad

Ingredients:

- 2 cups mixed greens
- 1/4 cup cooked and diced chicken breast
- 1 hard-boiled egg, chopped
- 1/4 cup diced tomato
- 1/4 cup diced cucumber
- 1/4 cup diced avocado
- 1/4 cup crumbled feta cheese
- 2 tablespoons extra-virgin olive oil
- 1 tablespoon red wine vinegar
- Salt and pepper, to taste

Instructions:

1. In a large salad bowl, combine the mixed greens, cooked and diced chicken breast, chopped hard-boiled egg, diced tomato, diced cucumber, diced avocado, and crumbled feta cheese.
2. In a small bowl, whisk together the extra-virgin olive oil and red wine vinegar to make the salad dressing.
3. Drizzle the salad dressing over the top of the salad.
4. Toss the salad gently to coat the ingredients with the dressing.

5. Season the Cobb salad with salt and pepper to taste.

6. Serve the Cobb salad immediately.

Cobb salad is a satisfying and nutritious meal for the Golo Diet. Mixed greens, chicken breast, hard-boiled egg, tomato, cucumber, avocado, and feta cheese are dressed with a simple olive oil and vinegar dressing. This recipe is customizable and perfect for meal prep or on-the-go lunches.

Cauliflower and Chickpea Tacos

Ingredients:

- 2 small corn tortillas
- 1/2 cup cooked chickpeas
- 1 cup chopped cauliflower florets
- 1/4 cup diced red onion
- 1/4 cup chopped cilantro
- 1 tablespoon extra-virgin olive oil
- 1/2 teaspoon chili powder
- 1/2 teaspoon cumin
- Salt and pepper, to taste
- Optional toppings: diced avocado, salsa, shredded cabbage

Instructions:

1. Preheat the oven to 400°F (200°C).
2. In a bowl, toss the chopped cauliflower florets with the extra-virgin olive oil, chili powder, cumin, salt, and pepper.
3. Spread the cauliflower florets out on a baking sheet and roast in the preheated oven for 15-20 minutes, or until the cauliflower is tender and slightly browned.
4. In a pan, heat the cooked chickpeas over medium-high heat.
5. Season the chickpeas with salt and pepper to taste.

6. Warm the corn tortillas in the microwave or in a pan over low heat.

7. Fill each warm tortilla with roasted cauliflower, cooked chickpeas, diced red onion, and chopped cilantro.

8. Serve the cauliflower and chickpea tacos with optional toppings, such as diced avocado, salsa, or shredded cabbage.

Roasted cauliflower and chickpeas make for a nutritious and flavorful taco filling. Diced red onion and cilantro add freshness. Customize with toppings such as avocado, salsa, or shredded cabbage. Perfect for the Golo Diet and easy to scale up.

Egg Salad Sandwich

Ingredients:

- 2 hard-boiled eggs, peeled and chopped
- 1 tablespoon diced red onion
- 1 tablespoon diced celery
- 1 tablespoon plain Greek yogurt
- 1 teaspoon Dijon mustard
- Salt and pepper, to taste
- 2 slices of whole grain bread
- 1 cup mixed greens

Instructions:

1. In a bowl, combine the chopped hard-boiled eggs, diced red onion, diced celery, plain Greek yogurt, Dijon mustard, salt, and pepper.
2. Mix the ingredients together until they are well-combined.
3. Toast the slices of whole grain bread.
4. Place the mixed greens on one slice of the toasted bread.
5. Spoon the egg salad mixture onto the mixed greens.
6. Top the egg salad with the other slice of toasted bread.
7. Cut the egg salad sandwich in half and serve.

This egg salad sandwich recipe is a delicious and satisfying lunch option that is perfect for the Golo Diet. Hard-boiled eggs provide protein and nutrients, while diced red onion and celery provide flavor and crunch. Plain Greek yogurt and Dijon mustard serve as a healthier alternative to mayonnaise, and add creaminess and tang to the egg salad mixture. Whole grain bread provides fiber and nutrients, while mixed greens add a serving of vegetables to the sandwich. This recipe can easily be customized with your favorite bread and vegetables, and can be prepared ahead of time for a quick and easy lunch option.

Dinner

Grilled Chicken and Vegetables

Ingredients:

- 4 oz boneless, skinless chicken breast
- 1/2 medium zucchini, sliced into rounds
- 1/2 medium red bell pepper, sliced into strips
- 1/2 medium red onion, sliced into wedges
- 1 tbsp olive oil
- 1/2 tsp dried basil
- 1/2 tsp dried oregano
- Salt and pepper to taste

Instructions:

1. Preheat a grill or grill pan to medium-high heat.
2. Season the chicken breast with salt and pepper on both sides.
3. In a bowl, toss the sliced zucchini, red bell pepper, and red onion with olive oil, dried basil, dried oregano, salt, and pepper.
4. Place the chicken breast on the grill and cook for 6-7 minutes on each side or until fully cooked. The internal temperature of the chicken should reach 165°F (74°C).

Dinner

5. While the chicken is cooking, grill the vegetables for 4-5 minutes on each side or until they are slightly charred and tender.

6. Once the chicken is fully cooked, remove it from the grill and let it rest for a few minutes before slicing it.

7. Serve the sliced chicken and grilled vegetables on a plate, garnished with additional dried herbs if desired.

This recipe is suitable for the Golo Diet as it is high in protein and low in carbohydrates. It's a healthy and delicious meal that's perfect for lunch or dinner. Enjoy!

Baked Salmon and Asparagus

Ingredients:

- 4 oz salmon fillet

- 1/2 bunch asparagus, ends trimmed

- 1 tbsp olive oil

- 1 garlic clove, minced

- Salt and pepper to taste

- 1/2 lemon, sliced

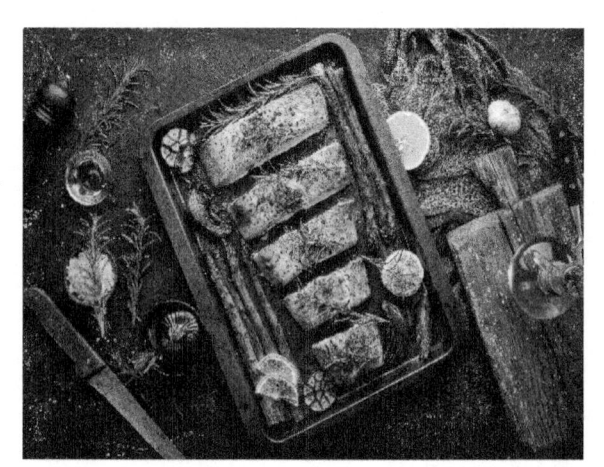

Instructions:

1. Preheat the oven to 400°F (200°C).

2. In a small bowl, mix together the olive oil, minced garlic, salt, and pepper.

3. Place the salmon fillet in the center of a piece of aluminum foil. Brush the salmon with the olive oil mixture and place lemon slices on top.

4. On either side of the salmon, place the trimmed asparagus. Brush with the remaining olive oil mixture.

5. Fold the edges of the aluminum foil together to create a packet, sealing the salmon and asparagus inside.

6. Place the foil packet on a baking sheet and bake for 12-15 minutes or until the salmon is cooked through and the asparagus is tender.

7. Carefully open the foil packet and transfer the salmon and asparagus to a plate.

8. Squeeze the juice from the lemon slices over the salmon and asparagus before serving.

Dinner

This recipe is suitable for the Golo Diet as it's low in carbohydrates and high in protein and healthy fats. It's a delicious and nutritious meal that's perfect for lunch or dinner. Enjoy!

Beef and Broccoli Stir-Fry

Ingredients:

- 4 oz flank steak, sliced into thin strips
- 1 cup broccoli florets
- 1 garlic clove, minced
- 1/2 inch ginger, grated
- 1 tbsp low-sodium soy sauce
- 1 tsp cornstarch
- 1 tsp sesame oil
- 1 tbsp vegetable oil
- Salt and pepper to taste

Instructions:

1. In a small bowl, whisk together the low-sodium soy sauce, cornstarch, and sesame oil.
2. Heat the vegetable oil in a large non-stick skillet or wok over medium-high heat.
3. Add the sliced flank steak to the skillet and cook for 2-3 minutes or until browned on all sides. Remove the steak from the skillet and set aside.
4. Add the broccoli florets, minced garlic, and grated ginger to the skillet. Cook for 2-3 minutes or until the broccoli is tender-crisp.
5. Add the cooked steak back to the skillet and pour in the soy sauce mixture. Stir to coat the beef and broccoli evenly.

Dinner

6. Cook for another minute or until the sauce has thickened and the beef is cooked to your desired doneness.

7. Serve the beef and broccoli stir-fry immediately, garnished with additional sliced green onions or sesame seeds if desired.

This recipe is suitable for the Golo Diet as it's low in carbohydrates and high in protein. It's a tasty and healthy meal that's perfect for lunch or dinner. Enjoy!

Roasted Vegetable Quinoa

Ingredients:

- 1/2 cup cooked quinoa
- 1/2 medium sweet potato, peeled and diced
- 1/2 medium zucchini, diced
- 1/2 red bell pepper, diced
- 1 garlic clove, minced
- 1 tbsp olive oil
- Salt and pepper to taste

Instructions:

1. Preheat the oven to 400°F (200°C).
2. In a bowl, toss the diced sweet potato, zucchini, and red bell pepper with the minced garlic, olive oil, salt, and pepper.
3. Spread the vegetables out in a single layer on a baking sheet and roast in the oven for 20-25 minutes or until the vegetables are tender and slightly charred.
4. In a separate bowl, mix together the cooked quinoa and the roasted vegetables.
5. Serve the Roasted Vegetable Quinoa immediately, garnished with additional fresh herbs or grated Parmesan cheese if desired.

This recipe is suitable for the Golo Diet as it's low in carbohydrates and high in fiber and nutrients. It's a flavorful and satisfying meal that's perfect for lunch or dinner. Enjoy!

Turkey Meatballs with Zucchini Noodles

Ingredients:

- 4 oz ground turkey
- 1/4 cup almond flour
- 1/4 cup grated Parmesan cheese
- 1 garlic clove, minced
- 1 egg
- 1 tsp dried oregano
- Salt and pepper to taste
- 1 medium zucchini, spiralized or cut into thin noodles
- 1 garlic clove, minced
- 1 tbsp olive oil
- Salt and pepper to taste

Instructions:

1. Preheat the oven to 375°F (190°C).

2. In a large bowl, mix together the ground turkey, almond flour, grated Parmesan cheese, minced garlic, egg, dried oregano, salt, and pepper.

3. Shape the mixture into 4-5 meatballs and place them on a baking sheet lined with parchment paper.

4. Bake the turkey meatballs in the oven for 15-20 minutes or until they are fully cooked and slightly browned.

5. While the turkey meatballs are baking, heat the olive oil in a large skillet over medium heat.

6. Add the minced garlic to the skillet and cook for 1-2 minutes or until fragrant.

7. Add the zucchini noodles to the skillet and toss to coat in the garlic and oil. Cook for 3-4 minutes or until the noodles are tender.

8. Serve the turkey meatballs on top of the zucchini noodles, garnished with additional grated Parmesan cheese and fresh herbs if desired.

This recipe is suitable for the Golo Diet as it's high in protein and low in carbohydrates. It's a delicious and healthy meal that's perfect for lunch or dinner. Enjoy!

Chicken and Veggie Sheet Pan Dinner

Ingredients:

- 4 oz boneless, skinless chicken breast
- 1/2 medium sweet potato, peeled and diced
- 1/2 medium zucchini, sliced into rounds
- 1/2 medium red bell pepper, sliced into strips
- 1/2 medium red onion, sliced into wedges
- 1 garlic clove, minced
- 1 tbsp olive oil
- 1 tsp dried thyme
- Salt and pepper to taste

Instructions:

1. Preheat the oven to 400°F (200°C).

2. Season the chicken breast with salt and pepper on both sides.

3. In a large bowl, toss the diced sweet potato, sliced zucchini, sliced red bell pepper, sliced red onion, minced garlic, olive oil, dried thyme, salt, and pepper.

4. Spread the vegetable mixture out in a single layer on a baking sheet.

5. Place the chicken breast on top of the vegetable mixture.

6. Bake the chicken and vegetables in the oven for 25-30 minutes or until the chicken is fully cooked and the vegetables are tender and slightly browned.

7. Serve the Chicken and Veggie Sheet Pan Dinner immediately, garnished with additional fresh herbs if desired.

This recipe is suitable for the Golo Diet as it's high in protein and fiber and low in carbohydrates. It's a quick and easy meal that's perfect for busy weeknights. Enjoy!

Dinner

Shrimp and Cauliflower Grits

Ingredients:

- 1/2 head cauliflower, cut into florets
- 1 garlic clove, minced
- 1 tbsp butter
- 1/4 cup grated Parmesan cheese
- Salt and pepper to taste
- 4 oz raw shrimp, peeled and deveined
- 1 garlic clove, minced
- 1 tbsp olive oil
- 1/4 tsp smoked paprika
- Salt and pepper to taste
- 1 tbsp chopped fresh parsley

Instructions:

1. In a large pot of boiling salted water, cook the cauliflower florets for 5-7 minutes or until they are tender.

2. Drain the cauliflower and transfer it to a food processor. Add the minced garlic, butter, grated Parmesan cheese, salt, and pepper. Puree until the mixture is smooth and creamy, similar to grits.

3. In a separate bowl, toss the peeled and deveined shrimp with minced garlic, olive oil, smoked paprika, salt, and pepper.

4. Heat a large skillet over medium-high heat. Add the seasoned shrimp to the skillet and cook for 2-3 minutes on each side or until they are pink and opaque.

5. Serve the cauliflower grits on a plate, topped with the cooked shrimp. Garnish with chopped fresh parsley.

This recipe is suitable for the Golo Diet as it's low in carbohydrates and high in protein and healthy fats. It's a delicious and satisfying meal that's perfect for lunch or dinner. Enjoy!

Dinner

Spinach and Feta Stuffed Chicken

Ingredients:

- 1 boneless, skinless chicken breast
- 1/4 cup frozen chopped spinach, thawed and drained
- 2 tbsp crumbled feta cheese
- 1 garlic clove, minced
- 1 tbsp olive oil
- Salt and pepper to taste

Instructions:

1. Preheat the oven to 375°F (190°C).

2. In a small bowl, mix together the chopped spinach, crumbled feta cheese, minced garlic, salt, and pepper.

3. Use a sharp knife to cut a slit in the thickest part of the chicken breast, creating a pocket for the stuffing.

4. Stuff the spinach and feta mixture into the pocket and use toothpicks to secure the chicken breast closed.

5. Heat the olive oil in a large oven-safe skillet over medium-high heat. Add the stuffed chicken breast to the skillet and cook for 2-3 minutes on each side or until it is browned on all sides.

6. Transfer the skillet to the oven and bake for 15-20 minutes or until the chicken is fully cooked and the internal temperature reaches 165°F (74°C).

7. Let the stuffed chicken breast rest for a few minutes before removing the toothpicks and slicing it.

8. Serve the Spinach and Feta Stuffed Chicken immediately, garnished with additional fresh herbs if desired.

This recipe is suitable for the Golo Diet as it's high in protein and low in carbohydrates. It's a delicious and healthy meal that's perfect for lunch or dinner. Enjoy!

Stuffed Portobello Mushrooms

Ingredients:

- 2 large Portobello mushrooms, stems removed
- 1/4 cup cooked quinoa
- 1/4 cup chopped spinach
- 1/4 cup diced tomatoes
- 2 tbsp crumbled feta cheese
- 1 garlic clove, minced
- 1 tbsp olive oil
- Salt and pepper to taste

Instructions:

1. Preheat the oven to 375°F (190°C).
2. In a small bowl, mix together the cooked quinoa, chopped spinach, diced tomatoes, crumbled feta cheese, minced garlic, salt, and pepper.
3. Place the Portobello mushrooms on a baking sheet lined with parchment paper.
4. Divide the quinoa mixture evenly between the two mushrooms, stuffing it into the caps.
5. Drizzle the stuffed mushrooms with olive oil and sprinkle with additional salt and pepper if desired.
6. Bake the stuffed mushrooms in the oven for 20-25 minutes or until the mushrooms are tender and the filling is hot and slightly browned.

7. Serve the Stuffed Portobello Mushrooms immediately, garnished with additional fresh herbs or grated Parmesan cheese if desired.

This recipe is suitable for the Golo Diet as it's low in carbohydrates and high in fiber and nutrients. It's a tasty and satisfying meal that's perfect for lunch or dinner. Enjoy!

Cilantro Lime Chicken and Rice

Ingredients:

- 4 oz boneless, skinless chicken breast
- 1/2 cup cooked brown rice
- 1/4 cup chopped fresh cilantro
- 1 garlic clove, minced
- 1 tbsp olive oil
- Juice of 1/2 lime
- Salt and pepper to taste

Instructions:

1. Season the chicken breast with salt and pepper on both sides.

2. Heat the olive oil in a large skillet over medium-high heat. Add the chicken breast to the skillet and cook for 5-6 minutes on each side or until it is browned and fully cooked.

3. Remove the chicken breast from the skillet and let it rest for a few minutes before slicing it into thin strips.

4. In a small bowl, mix together the chopped fresh cilantro, minced garlic, lime juice, salt, and pepper.

5. In the same skillet used to cook the chicken, add the cooked brown rice and stir to heat it up.

6. Add the sliced chicken to the skillet with the rice and stir to combine.

7. Pour the cilantro lime mixture over the chicken and rice, stirring to coat everything evenly.

8. Serve the Cilantro Lime Chicken and Rice immediately, garnished with additional chopped cilantro if desired.

This recipe is suitable for the Golo Diet as it's high in protein and fiber and low in carbohydrates. It's a flavorful and nutritious meal that's perfect for lunch or dinner. Enjoy!

Eggplant Parmesan

Ingredients:

- 1 small eggplant, sliced into rounds
- 1/4 cup almond flour
- 1/4 cup grated Parmesan cheese
- 1 egg
- 1/2 cup low-sugar marinara sauce
- 1/4 cup shredded mozzarella cheese
- 1 tbsp olive oil
- Salt and pepper to taste

Instructions:

1. Preheat the oven to 375°F (190°C).
2. In a shallow dish, whisk together the almond flour and grated Parmesan cheese.
3. In a separate dish, beat the egg.
4. Dip each eggplant slice into the beaten egg, then coat it in the almond flour and Parmesan mixture.
5. Heat the olive oil in a large skillet over medium heat. Add the coated eggplant slices to the skillet and cook for 2-3 minutes on each side or until they are browned and crispy.
6. Remove the eggplant slices from the skillet and transfer them to a baking dish.

7. Spread the low-sugar marinara sauce over the top of the eggplant slices.

8. Sprinkle the shredded mozzarella cheese on top of the marinara sauce.

9. Bake the Eggplant Parmesan in the oven for 15-20 minutes or until the cheese is melted and bubbly.

10. Serve the Eggplant Parmesan immediately, garnished with additional fresh herbs if desired.

This recipe is suitable for the Golo Diet as it's low in carbohydrates and high in fiber and nutrients. It's a delicious and healthy meal that's perfect for lunch or dinner. Enjoy!

Ground Turkey Lettuce Wraps

Ingredients:

- 4 oz ground turkey
- 1 garlic clove, minced
- 1/4 cup diced red bell pepper
- 2 tbsp diced onion
- 1 tbsp olive oil
- 1 tbsp low-sodium soy sauce
- 1 tbsp hoisin sauce
- 1/4 tsp ground ginger
- Salt and pepper to taste
- 4-5 large lettuce leaves

Instructions:

1. Heat the olive oil in a large skillet over medium-high heat. Add the minced garlic, diced red bell pepper, and diced onion to the skillet and cook for 2-3 minutes or until the vegetables are slightly softened.

2. Add the ground turkey to the skillet and cook for 5-6 minutes, breaking it up into small pieces with a spatula, until it's fully cooked and browned.

3. In a small bowl, mix together the low-sodium soy sauce, hoisin sauce, ground ginger, salt, and pepper.

4. Add the sauce mixture to the skillet with the cooked turkey and vegetables. Stir to coat everything evenly and cook for an additional 1-2 minutes.

5. Wash and dry the lettuce leaves and arrange them on a plate.

6. Spoon the turkey mixture into the lettuce leaves, using them as wraps.

7. Serve the Ground Turkey Lettuce Wraps immediately, garnished with additional fresh herbs or chopped peanuts if desired.

This recipe is suitable for the Golo Diet as it's high in protein and low in carbohydrates. It's a flavorful and satisfying meal that's perfect for lunch or dinner. Enjoy!

Dinner

Black Bean and Sweet Potato Chili

Ingredients:

- 1/2 small sweet potato, peeled and diced

- 1/4 cup diced onion

- 1 garlic clove, minced

- 1/2 cup low-sodium vegetable broth

- 1/2 cup canned black beans, rinsed and drained

- 1/2 cup canned diced tomatoes

- 1/4 tsp chili powder

- 1/4 tsp ground cumin

- Salt and pepper to taste

- Optional toppings: chopped fresh cilantro, diced avocado, shredded cheese, sour cream

Instructions:

1. In a large pot, heat the vegetable broth over medium-high heat. Add the diced sweet potato, diced onion, and minced garlic to the pot and cook for 5-7 minutes or until the vegetables are slightly softened.

2. Add the canned black beans, canned diced tomatoes, chili powder, ground cumin, salt, and pepper to the pot. Stir everything together and bring the chili to a simmer.

3. Reduce the heat to low and let the chili cook for 15-20 minutes or until the sweet potatoes are tender and the flavors have melded together.

4. Serve the Black Bean and Sweet Potato Chili immediately, garnished with chopped fresh cilantro, diced avocado, shredded cheese, or sour cream if desired.

This recipe is suitable for the Golo Diet as it's high in fiber and nutrients and low in fat and calories. It's a warming and satisfying meal that's perfect for lunch or dinner. Enjoy!

Baked Cod with Tomatoes and Olives

Ingredients:

- 4 oz cod fillet
- 1/2 cup cherry tomatoes, halved
- 1/4 cup sliced Kalamata olives
- 1 garlic clove, minced
- 1 tbsp olive oil
- 1/2 tbsp chopped fresh parsley
- Salt and pepper to taste

Instructions:

1. Preheat the oven to 375°F (190°C).
2. In a small bowl, mix together the halved cherry tomatoes, sliced Kalamata olives, minced garlic, chopped fresh parsley, salt, and pepper.
3. Place the cod fillet in a small baking dish and drizzle it with olive oil.
4. Spoon the tomato and olive mixture over the top of the cod fillet, spreading it evenly.
5. Bake the Baked Cod with Tomatoes and Olives in the oven for 15-20 minutes or until the cod is fully cooked and opaque.
6. Serve the Baked Cod with Tomatoes and Olives immediately, garnished with additional fresh herbs if desired.

This recipe is suitable for the Golo Diet as it's high in protein and healthy fats and low in carbohydrates. It's a flavorful and nutritious meal that's perfect for lunch or dinner. Enjoy!

Chicken, Mushroom, and Spinach Skillet

Ingredients:

- 4 oz boneless, skinless chicken breast, sliced into strips
- 1/2 cup sliced mushrooms
- 1 cup fresh spinach leaves
- 1 garlic clove, minced
- 1 tbsp olive oil
- Salt and pepper to taste

Instructions:

1. Heat the olive oil in a large skillet over medium-high heat. Add the sliced chicken breast to the skillet and cook for 5-6 minutes, stirring occasionally, or until it's browned and fully cooked.

2. Add the sliced mushrooms and minced garlic to the skillet with the cooked chicken. Cook for 2-3 minutes or until the mushrooms are slightly softened.

3. Add the fresh spinach leaves to the skillet and stir everything together. Cook for an additional 1-2 minutes or until the spinach is wilted.

4. Season the Chicken, Mushroom, and Spinach Skillet with salt and pepper to taste.

5. Serve the Chicken, Mushroom, and Spinach Skillet immediately, garnished with additional fresh herbs or grated Parmesan cheese if desired.

This recipe is suitable for the Golo Diet as it's high in protein and nutrients and low in carbohydrates. It's a simple and delicious meal that's perfect for lunch or dinner. Enjoy!

Slow Cooker Pulled Pork

Ingredients:

- 4 oz pork shoulder, trimmed of excess fat
- 1/4 cup low-sugar barbecue sauce
- 1/4 tsp smoked paprika
- 1/4 tsp garlic powder
- Salt and pepper to taste

Instructions:

1. Rub the trimmed pork shoulder with smoked paprika, garlic powder, salt, and pepper on all sides.

2. Place the seasoned pork shoulder in a slow cooker and pour the low-sugar barbecue sauce over the top of it.

3. Cover the slow cooker and cook the pork shoulder on low heat for 6-8 hours or until the pork is fully cooked and tender.

4. Remove the pork from the slow cooker and use two forks to shred it into small pieces.

5. Serve the Slow Cooker Pulled Pork immediately, garnished with additional low-sugar barbecue sauce or fresh herbs if desired.

This recipe is suitable for the Golo Diet as it's high in protein and low in carbohydrates. It's a delicious and easy meal that's perfect for lunch or dinner. Enjoy!

Vegetable Stir-Fry with Tofu

Ingredients:

- 4 oz firm tofu, pressed and cut into cubes
- 1/2 cup sliced mixed vegetables
- 1 garlic clove, minced
- 1 tbsp low-sodium soy sauce
- 1 tbsp rice vinegar
- 1 tsp honey or maple syrup
- 1/4 tsp ground ginger
- 1/4 tsp cornstarch
- 1 tbsp olive oil
- Salt and pepper to taste

Instructions:

1. Heat the olive oil in a large skillet over medium-high heat. Add the cubed tofu to the skillet and cook for 3-4 minutes on each side or until it's browned and crispy.

2. Remove the cooked tofu from the skillet and set it aside.

3. Add the sliced mixed vegetables and minced garlic to the skillet and cook for 2-3 minutes or until the vegetables are slightly softened.

4. In a small bowl, whisk together the low-sodium soy sauce, rice vinegar, honey or maple syrup, ground ginger, cornstarch, salt, and pepper.

Dinner

5. Pour the sauce mixture into the skillet with the cooked vegetables and stir everything together.

6. Add the cooked tofu back to the skillet and stir to coat it in the sauce.

7. Cook the Vegetable Stir-Fry with Tofu for an additional 1-2 minutes or until the sauce has thickened and the tofu and vegetables are coated.

8. Serve the Vegetable Stir-Fry with Tofu immediately, garnished with additional fresh herbs or chopped peanuts if desired.

This recipe is suitable for the Golo Diet as it's high in protein and fiber and low in carbohydrates. It's a healthy and flavorful meal that's perfect for lunch or dinner. Enjoy!

Chicken Piccata

Ingredients:

- 4 oz boneless, skinless chicken breast, pounded thin
- 1 tbsp almond flour
- 1/4 cup low-sodium chicken broth
- 1/4 cup canned diced tomatoes
- 1 garlic clove, minced
- 1 tbsp capers
- 1 tbsp lemon juice
- 1 tbsp olive oil
- Salt and pepper to taste
- Optional garnish: chopped fresh parsley

Instructions:

1. Season the pounded chicken breast with salt and pepper on both sides, then dredge it in almond flour to coat.

2. Heat the olive oil in a large skillet over medium-high heat. Add the coated chicken breast to the skillet and cook for 3-4 minutes on each side or until it's browned and fully cooked.

3. Remove the cooked chicken breast from the skillet and set it aside.

Dinner

4. In the same skillet, add the low-sodium chicken broth, canned diced tomatoes (with their juices), minced garlic, and capers. Stir everything together and bring the mixture to a simmer.

5. Add the lemon juice to the skillet and stir to combine.

6. Return the cooked chicken breast to the skillet and spoon the sauce over the top of it.

7. Cook the Chicken Piccata for an additional 1-2 minutes or until the sauce has thickened slightly and the chicken breast is coated.

8. Serve the Chicken Piccata immediately, garnished with chopped fresh parsley if desired.

This recipe is suitable for the Golo Diet as it's high in protein and healthy fats and low in carbohydrates. It's a delicious and satisfying meal that's perfect for lunch or dinner. Enjoy!

Pork Tenderloin with Roasted Vegetables

Ingredients:

- 4 oz pork tenderloin
- 1/2 cup mixed vegetables, chopped
- 1 garlic clove, minced
- 1 tbsp olive oil
- Salt and pepper to taste

Instructions:

1. Preheat the oven to 375°F (190°C).
2. In a small bowl, mix together the minced garlic, olive oil, salt, and pepper.
3. Place the pork tenderloin in a baking dish and rub the garlic and olive oil mixture all over it.
4. Arrange the chopped mixed vegetables around the pork tenderloin in the baking dish.
5. Roast the Pork Tenderloin with Roasted Vegetables in the oven for 20-25 minutes or until the pork is fully cooked and the vegetables are tender.
6. Remove the baking dish from the oven and let the pork rest for 5 minutes before slicing it into thin pieces.
7. Serve the Pork Tenderloin with Roasted Vegetables immediately, with the roasted vegetables on the side or on top of the sliced pork.

This recipe is suitable for the Golo Diet as it's high in protein and nutrients and low in carbohydrates. It's a simple and flavorful meal that's perfect for lunch or dinner. Enjoy!

Seared Scallops with Cauliflower Puree

Ingredients:

- 4 large sea scallops
- 1/2 head of cauliflower, chopped
- 1 garlic clove, minced
- 1 tbsp olive oil
- Salt and pepper to taste
- Optional garnish: chopped fresh herbs

Instructions:

1. Bring a pot of salted water to a boil. Add the chopped cauliflower to the pot and cook for 5-7 minutes or until it's tender.

2. Drain the cooked cauliflower and transfer it to a food processor or blender. Add the minced garlic, olive oil, salt, and pepper to the cauliflower and blend until it's smooth and creamy.

3. Heat a large skillet over medium-high heat. Add the sea scallops to the skillet and cook for 2-3 minutes on each side or until they're browned and fully cooked.

4. Divide the Cauliflower Puree between two plates, spreading it out into a thin layer.

5. Place two cooked scallops on top of the Cauliflower Puree on each plate.

6. Serve the Seared Scallops with Cauliflower Puree immediately, garnished with chopped fresh herbs if desired.

This recipe is suitable for the Golo Diet as it's high in protein and nutrients and low in carbohydrates. It's a decadent and satisfying meal that's perfect for a special occasion or a fancy dinner. Enjoy!

Snacks and Appetizers

Veggie Sticks with Hummus

Ingredients:

- 1/2 cup mixed vegetables, cut into sticks

- 1/4 cup low-fat or fat-free hummus

Instructions:

1. Wash and cut the mixed vegetables into sticks.

2. Serve the Veggie Sticks with Hummus on a plate or in a bowl, with the hummus on the side for dipping.

3. Enjoy the Veggie Sticks with Hummus immediately as a healthy and delicious snack.

This recipe is suitable for the Golo Diet as it's low in calories and carbohydrates and high in fiber and nutrients. It's a great option for a quick and easy snack or a light lunch. Enjoy!

Snacks and Appetizers

Baked Kale Chips

Ingredients:

- 1/2 bunch kale, stems removed and leaves torn into bite-sized pieces

- 1 tsp olive oil

- Salt and pepper to taste

Instructions:

1. Preheat the oven to 350°F (175°C).

2. Wash the kale leaves and pat them dry with a paper towel. Remove the stems and tear the leaves into bite-sized pieces.

3. In a large bowl, toss the kale pieces with olive oil, salt, and pepper until they're coated evenly.

4. Spread the seasoned kale pieces out in a single layer on a baking sheet.

5. Bake the Baked Kale Chips in the oven for 10-15 minutes or until they're crispy and slightly browned.

6. Remove the baking sheet from the oven and let the kale chips cool for a few minutes before serving.

7. Serve the Baked Kale Chips immediately as a healthy and delicious snack.

This recipe is suitable for the Golo Diet as it's low in calories and carbohydrates and high in fiber and nutrients. It's a great option for a quick and easy snack or a light lunch. Enjoy!

Apple Slices with Almond Butter

Ingredients:

- 1 medium apple, cored and sliced
- 1 tbsp almond butter

Instructions:

1. Wash the apple and cut it into thin slices.
2. Spread the almond butter on a small plate or in a small bowl.
3. Serve the Apple Slices with Almond Butter by dipping the apple slices into the almond butter and enjoying them immediately.

This recipe is suitable for the Golo Diet as it's low in calories and carbohydrates and high in fiber and healthy fats. It's a great option for a quick and easy snack or a light breakfast. Enjoy!

Greek Salad Skewers

Ingredients:

- 1/2 cup cherry tomatoes
- 1/2 cup cucumber, chopped
- 1/4 cup feta cheese, crumbled
- 2 tbsp red onion, chopped
- 1 tbsp olive oil
- 1 tbsp lemon juice
- 1/2 tsp dried oregano
- Salt and pepper to taste
- 2 skewers

Instructions:

1. Wash the cherry tomatoes and chop the cucumber into bite-sized pieces.
2. Thread the cherry tomatoes, cucumber, feta cheese, and red onion onto the skewers in any order you like.
3. In a small bowl, whisk together the olive oil, lemon juice, dried oregano, salt, and pepper to make the dressing.
4. Drizzle the dressing over the Greek Salad Skewers.
5. Serve the Greek Salad Skewers immediately as a healthy and delicious snack or appetizer.

This recipe is suitable for the Golo Diet as it's low in calories and carbohydrates and high in fiber and nutrients. It's a great option for a quick and easy snack or a light lunch. Enjoy!

Spicy Roasted Chickpeas

Ingredients:

- 1/2 cup cooked chickpeas
- 1 tsp olive oil
- 1/4 tsp ground cumin
- 1/4 tsp paprika
- 1/8 tsp cayenne pepper
- Salt and pepper to taste

Instructions:

1. Preheat the oven to 375°F (190°C).
2. Rinse the cooked chickpeas and pat them dry with a paper towel.
3. In a small bowl, mix together the olive oil, ground cumin, paprika, cayenne pepper, salt, and pepper.
4. Toss the chickpeas in the spice mixture until they're coated evenly.
5. Spread the seasoned chickpeas out in a single layer on a baking sheet.
6. Bake the Spicy Roasted Chickpeas in the oven for 15-20 minutes or until they're crispy and slightly browned.
7. Remove the baking sheet from the oven and let the chickpeas cool for a few minutes before serving.
8. Serve the Spicy Roasted Chickpeas immediately as a healthy and delicious snack.

Snacks and Appetizers

This recipe is suitable for the Golo Diet as it's low in calories and carbohydrates and high in fiber and protein. It's a great option for a quick and easy snack or a light lunch. Enjoy!

Mini Caprese Bites

Ingredients:

- 6 cherry tomatoes, halved
- 6 mini fresh mozzarella balls
- 6 small basil leaves
- 1 tbsp balsamic vinegar
- 1 tbsp olive oil
- Salt and pepper to taste
- 6 toothpicks

Instructions:

1. Wash the cherry tomatoes and pat them dry with a paper towel. Cut them in half.
2. Drain the mini fresh mozzarella balls.
3. Wash the basil leaves and pat them dry with a paper towel.
4. Thread one cherry tomato half, one mini fresh mozzarella ball, and one small basil leaf onto each toothpick in any order you like.
5. In a small bowl, whisk together the balsamic vinegar, olive oil, salt, and pepper to make the dressing.
6. Drizzle the dressing over the Mini Caprese Bites.
7. Serve the Mini Caprese Bites immediately as a healthy and delicious snack or appetizer.

This recipe is suitable for the Golo Diet as it's low in calories and carbohydrates and high in fiber and nutrients. It's a great option for a quick and easy snack or a light lunch. Enjoy!

Snacks and Appetizers

Zucchini Fritters

Ingredients:

- 1 medium zucchini, grated
- 1 egg
- 2 tbsp almond flour
- 1/4 tsp garlic powder
- 1/4 tsp onion powder
- Salt and pepper to taste
- 1 tbsp olive oil
- Optional garnish: chopped fresh herbs

Instructions:

1. Wash the zucchini and grate it using a cheese grater or food processor.
2. Place the grated zucchini in a clean kitchen towel and squeeze out any excess liquid.
3. In a large bowl, whisk together the egg, almond flour, garlic powder, onion powder, salt, and pepper.
4. Add the grated zucchini to the bowl and mix well.
5. Heat the olive oil in a large skillet over medium heat.
6. Spoon the zucchini mixture into the skillet in 1/4 cup portions and flatten each one into a fritter shape.

7. Cook the Zucchini Fritters for 2-3 minutes on each side or until they're golden brown and fully cooked.

8. Cook the Zucchini Fritters for 2-3 minutes on each side or until they're golden brown and fully cooked.

9. Serve the Zucchini Fritters immediately, garnished with chopped fresh herbs if desired.

This recipe is suitable for the Golo Diet as it's low in calories and carbohydrates and high in fiber and nutrients. It's a great option for a quick and easy snack or a light lunch. Enjoy!

Snacks and Appetizers

Smoked Salmon Cucumber Bites

Ingredients:

- 4-5 slices of cucumber, cut into rounds
- 2 oz smoked salmon, cut into small pieces
- 1 tbsp cream cheese
- 1 tsp fresh dill, chopped
- Salt and pepper to taste

Instructions:

1. Wash the cucumber and cut it into rounds, about 1/4 inch thick.
2. In a small bowl, mix together the cream cheese, fresh dill, salt, and pepper.
3. Spread a small amount of the cream cheese mixture onto each cucumber round.
4. Top each cucumber round with a small piece of smoked salmon.
5. Garnish the Smoked Salmon Cucumber Bites with additional fresh dill, if desired.
6. Serve the Smoked Salmon Cucumber Bites immediately as a healthy and delicious snack or appetizer.

This recipe is suitable for the Golo Diet as it's low in calories and carbohydrates and high in protein and healthy fats. It's a great option for a quick and easy snack or a light lunch. Enjoy!

Almond Stuffed Dates

Ingredients:

- 4 Medjool dates, pitted
- 4 whole almonds
- Optional toppings: shredded coconut, cinnamon

Instructions:

1. Wash the Medjool dates and remove the pits using a small knife.
2. Stuff each date with one whole almond, pressing it into the center of the date.
3. Optional: Roll the stuffed dates in shredded coconut or sprinkle with cinnamon for extra flavor.
4. Serve the Almond Stuffed Dates immediately as a healthy and delicious snack or dessert.

This recipe is suitable for the Golo Diet as it's low in calories and carbohydrates and high in fiber and healthy fats. It's a great option for a quick and easy snack or a sweet treat. Enjoy!

Snacks and Appetizers

Turkey and Cheese Roll-Ups

Ingredients:

- 3-4 slices of roasted turkey breast
- 2 slices of cheddar cheese
- 1/4 cup baby spinach leaves
- Mustard or mayonnaise
- Toothpicks

Instructions:

1. Lay out the slices of roasted turkey breast on a clean surface.
2. Place one slice of cheddar cheese on each slice of turkey.
3. Top each slice of cheese with a few baby spinach leaves.
4. Optional: Spread a small amount of mustard or mayonnaise on each slice of turkey for extra flavor.
5. Roll up each slice of turkey tightly and secure it with a toothpick.
6. Serve the Turkey and Cheese Roll-Ups immediately as a healthy and delicious snack or light lunch.

This recipe is suitable for the Golo Diet as it's low in calories and carbohydrates and high in protein and healthy fats. It's a great option for a quick and easy snack or a light lunch. Enjoy!

Baked Sweet Potato Fries

Ingredients:

- 1 small sweet potato, peeled and cut into thin fries
- 1 tsp olive oil
- 1/4 tsp garlic powder
- 1/4 tsp paprika
- Salt and pepper to taste

Instructions:

1. Preheat the oven to 400°F (200°C).
2. Wash the sweet potato and peel it.
3. Cut the sweet potato into thin fries, about 1/4 inch thick.
4. In a small bowl, mix together the olive oil, garlic powder, paprika, salt, and pepper.
5. Toss the sweet potato fries in the spice mixture until they're coated evenly.
6. Spread the seasoned sweet potato fries out in a single layer on a baking sheet.
7. Bake the Baked Sweet Potato Fries in the oven for 20-25 minutes or until they're crispy and slightly browned.
8. Remove the baking sheet from the oven and let the sweet potato fries cool for a few minutes before serving.
9. Serve the Baked Sweet Potato Fries immediately as a healthy and delicious snack or side dish.

Snacks and Appetizers

This recipe is suitable for the Golo Diet as it's low in calories and carbohydrates and high in fiber and nutrients. It's a great option for a quick and easy snack or a side dish. Enjoy!

Guacamole with Bell Pepper Dippers

Ingredients:

- 1 ripe avocado, pitted and mashed
- 1/4 small red onion, finely chopped
- 1 small garlic clove, minced
- 1/2 small jalapeño pepper, seeded and minced
- 1 tbsp lime juice
- Salt and pepper to taste
- 1 small bell pepper, sliced into strips
- 1/4 tsp garlic powder
- 1/4 tsp paprika
- Salt and pepper to taste

Instructions:

1. In a small bowl, mix together the mashed avocado, chopped red onion, minced garlic clove, minced jalapeño pepper, lime juice, salt, and pepper until well combined.

2. Cover the bowl with plastic wrap and refrigerate for at least 30 minutes to allow the flavors to blend.

3. Wash the bell pepper and slice it into thin strips.

Snacks and Appetizers

4. In a small bowl, mix together the garlic powder, paprika, salt, and pepper.

5. Toss the bell pepper strips in the spice mixture until they're coated evenly.

6. Serve the Guacamole with the Bell Pepper Dippers immediately as a healthy and delicious snack or appetizer.

This recipe is suitable for the Golo Diet as it's low in calories and carbohydrates and high in fiber and nutrients. It's a great option for a quick and easy snack or a light appetizer. Enjoy!

Antipasto Skewers

Ingredients:

- 3 cherry tomatoes
- 3 slices of salami
- 3 cubes of mozzarella cheese
- 3 slices of cucumber
- 3 pitted olives
- 1 tbsp balsamic vinegar
- 1 tsp olive oil
- Salt and pepper to taste
- 3 toothpicks

Instructions:

1. Wash the cherry tomatoes and cucumber and slice them into thin rounds.
2. Cut the slices of salami and mozzarella cheese into small cubes.
3. Thread the cherry tomatoes, salami, mozzarella cheese, cucumber, and olives onto the toothpicks, alternating the ingredients as desired.
4. In a small bowl, mix together the balsamic vinegar, olive oil, salt, and pepper to make a simple dressing.
5. Drizzle the dressing over the Antipasto Skewers before serving.
6. Serve the Antipasto Skewers immediately as a healthy and delicious snack or appetizer.

Snacks and Appetizers

This recipe is suitable for the Golo Diet as it's low in calories and carbohydrates and high in protein and healthy fats. It's a great option for a quick and easy snack or a light appetizer. Enjoy!

Deviled Eggs

Ingredients:

- 2 hard-boiled eggs, peeled
- 1 tbsp mayonnaise
- 1 tsp Dijon mustard
- 1/4 tsp paprika
- Salt and pepper to taste
- Optional toppings: chopped chives, sliced jalapeño

Instructions:

1. Cut the hard-boiled eggs in half lengthwise and remove the yolks.
2. In a small bowl, mash the egg yolks with a fork until they're smooth.
3. Add the mayonnaise, Dijon mustard, paprika, salt, and pepper to the bowl and mix well.
4. Spoon the egg yolk mixture back into the egg white halves, dividing it evenly between them.
5. Optional: Garnish the Deviled Eggs with chopped chives or sliced jalapeño for extra flavor.
6. Serve the Deviled Eggs immediately as a healthy and delicious snack or appetizer.

This recipe is suitable for the Golo Diet as it's low in calories and carbohydrates and high in protein and healthy fats. It's a great option for a quick and easy snack or a light appetizer. Enjoy!

Side Dishes

Garlic Green Beans

Ingredients:

- 1 cup fresh green beans, washed and trimmed
- 1 clove garlic, minced
- 1 tsp olive oil
- Salt and pepper to taste

Instructions:

1. Bring a pot of salted water to a boil over high heat.
2. Add the green beans to the boiling water and cook for 2-3 minutes or until they're crisp-tender.
3. Drain the green beans and rinse them under cold water to stop the cooking process.
4. In a large skillet, heat the olive oil over medium heat.
5. Add the minced garlic to the skillet and sauté for 1-2 minutes or until it's fragrant and slightly browned.
6. Add the green beans to the skillet and toss them in the garlic and olive oil until they're coated evenly.
7. Season the Garlic Green Beans with salt and pepper to taste.
8. Serve the Garlic Green Beans immediately as a healthy and delicious side dish.

This recipe is suitable for the Golo Diet as it's low in calories and carbohydrates and high in fiber and nutrients. It's a great option for a quick and easy side dish to accompany any meal. Enjoy!

Side Dishes

Quinoa Pilaf

Ingredients:

- 1/2 cup quinoa, rinsed and drained
- 1/2 cup low-sodium chicken or vegetable broth
- 1/4 small onion, diced
- 1 clove garlic, minced
- 1/4 cup chopped carrots
- 1/4 cup chopped red bell pepper
- 1/4 cup chopped zucchini
- 1/2 tbsp olive oil
- Salt and pepper to taste

Instructions:

1. In a small saucepan, bring the chicken or vegetable broth to a boil over high heat.

2. Add the quinoa to the boiling broth and reduce the heat to low.

3. Cover the saucepan with a tight-fitting lid and simmer the quinoa for 15-20 minutes or until it's tender and the liquid has been absorbed.

4. While the quinoa is cooking, heat the olive oil in a separate skillet over medium heat.

5. Add the diced onion and minced garlic to the skillet and sauté for 1-2 minutes or until they're slightly browned and fragrant.

6. Add the chopped carrots, red bell pepper, and zucchini to the skillet and continue to sauté for 5-7 minutes or until the vegetables are tender.

7. Season the Vegetable Quinoa Pilaf with salt and pepper to taste.

8. Serve the Vegetable Quinoa Pilaf immediately as a healthy and delicious side dish.

This recipe is suitable for the Golo Diet as it's low in calories and carbohydrates and high in fiber and nutrients. It's a great option for a quick and easy side dish to accompany any meal. Enjoy!

Side Dishes

Roasted Brussels Sprouts

Ingredients:

- 1 cup Brussels sprouts, trimmed and halved
- 1 tbsp olive oil
- 1 clove garlic, minced
- Salt and pepper to taste

Instructions:

1. Preheat your oven to 400°F (200°C).
2. Line a baking sheet with parchment paper or aluminum foil.
3. In a small bowl, mix together the olive oil, minced garlic, salt, and pepper.
4. Add the halved Brussels sprouts to the bowl and toss them in the olive oil mixture until they're coated evenly.
5. Spread the Brussels sprouts out in a single layer on the prepared baking sheet.
6. Roast the Brussels sprouts in the preheated oven for 20-25 minutes or until they're tender and browned on the outside.
7. Serve the Roasted Brussels Sprouts immediately as a healthy and delicious side dish.

This recipe is suitable for the Golo Diet as it's low in calories and carbohydrates and high in fiber and nutrients. It's a great option for a quick and easy side dish to accompany any meal. Enjoy!

Grilled Asparagus

Ingredients:

- 6-8 asparagus spears, washed and trimmed
- 1/2 tbsp olive oil
- Salt and pepper to taste

Instructions:

1. Preheat your grill or grill pan to medium-high heat.
2. In a small bowl, mix together the olive oil, salt, and pepper.
3. Brush the asparagus spears with the olive oil mixture, making sure they're coated evenly.
4. Place the asparagus spears on the grill or grill pan and cook for 2-3 minutes per side or until they're tender and lightly charred.
5. Remove the grilled asparagus from the grill or grill pan and serve immediately.

This recipe is suitable for the Golo Diet as it's low in calories and carbohydrates and high in fiber and nutrients. It's a great option for a quick and easy side dish to accompany any meal. Enjoy!

Side Dishes

Cauliflower Rice

Ingredients:

- 1/2 head cauliflower, chopped into florets
- 1 tbsp olive oil
- 1/4 small onion, diced
- 1 clove garlic, minced
- Salt and pepper to taste

Instructions:

1. Place the cauliflower florets in a food processor and pulse until they're finely chopped and resemble rice.

2. In a large skillet, heat the olive oil over medium heat.

3. Add the diced onion and minced garlic to the skillet and sauté for 1-2 minutes or until they're slightly browned and fragrant.

4. Add the cauliflower rice to the skillet and toss it in the onion and garlic until it's coated evenly.

5. Sauté the cauliflower rice for 3-5 minutes or until it's tender and slightly browned.

6. Season the Cauliflower Rice with salt and pepper to taste.

7. Serve the Cauliflower Rice immediately as a healthy and delicious side dish.

This recipe is suitable for the Golo Diet as it's low in calories and carbohydrates and high in fiber and nutrients. It's a great option for a quick and easy side dish to accompany any meal. Enjoy!

Balsamic Glazed Carrots

Ingredients:

- 1 cup baby carrots, washed and peeled
- 1 tbsp olive oil
- 1 tbsp balsamic vinegar
- 1 tsp honey
- Salt and pepper to taste

Instructions:

1. In a small bowl, whisk together the olive oil, balsamic vinegar, honey, salt, and pepper.

2. In a medium saucepan, bring water to a boil over high heat.

3. Add the baby carrots to the boiling water and cook for 4-5 minutes or until they're tender.

4. Drain the carrots and return them to the saucepan.

5. Pour the balsamic glaze over the carrots and toss them in the glaze until they're coated evenly.

6. Heat the carrots and balsamic glaze over low heat for 1-2 minutes or until the glaze thickens slightly and the carrots are glazed.

7. Serve the Balsamic Glazed Carrots immediately as a healthy and delicious side dish.

This recipe is suitable for the Golo Diet as it's low in calories and carbohydrates and high in fiber and nutrients. It's a great option for a quick and easy side dish to accompany any meal. Enjoy!

Side Dishes

Lemon Herb Couscous

Ingredients:

- 1/2 cup cooked couscous
- 1/2 tbsp olive oil
- 1/4 small onion, diced
- 1 clove garlic, minced
- 1 tbsp fresh lemon juice
- 1 tbsp chopped fresh parsley
- Salt and pepper to taste

Instructions:

1. Cook the couscous according to the package directions.
2. In a medium skillet, heat the olive oil over medium heat.
3. Add the diced onion and minced garlic to the skillet and sauté for 1-2 minutes or until they're slightly browned and fragrant.
4. Add the cooked couscous to the skillet and toss it in the onion and garlic until it's coated evenly.
5. Drizzle the fresh lemon juice over the couscous and toss it to distribute evenly.
6. Add the chopped fresh parsley to the skillet and toss everything together.
7. Season the Lemon Herb Couscous with salt and pepper to taste.
8. Serve the Lemon Herb Couscous immediately as a healthy and delicious side dish.

This recipe is suitable for the Golo Diet as it's low in calories and carbohydrates and high in fiber and nutrients. It's a great option for a quick and easy side dish to accompany any meal. Enjoy!

Side Dishes

Cilantro Lime Rice

Ingredients:

- 1/2 cup cooked brown rice
- 1/2 tbsp olive oil
- 1/4 small onion, diced
- 1 clove garlic, minced
- 1 tbsp fresh lime juice
- 1 tbsp chopped fresh cilantro
- Salt and pepper to taste

Instructions:

1. Cook the brown rice according to the package directions.
2. In a medium skillet, heat the olive oil over medium heat.
3. Add the diced onion and minced garlic to the skillet and sauté for 1-2 minutes or until they're slightly browned and fragrant.
4. Add the cooked brown rice to the skillet and toss it in the onion and garlic until it's coated evenly.
5. Drizzle the fresh lime juice over the rice and toss it to distribute evenly.
6. Add the chopped fresh cilantro to the skillet and toss everything together.
7. Season the Cilantro Lime Rice with salt and pepper to taste.
8. Serve the Cilantro Lime Rice immediately as a healthy and delicious side dish.

This recipe is suitable for the Golo Diet as it's low in calories and carbohydrates and high in fiber and nutrients. It's a great option for a quick and easy side dish to accompany any meal. Enjoy!

Steamed Broccoli with Lemon

Ingredients:

- 1 cup broccoli florets
- 1/2 tbsp olive oil
- 1/2 tbsp fresh lemon juice
- Salt and pepper to taste

Instructions:

1. Bring a small pot of water to a boil over high heat.
2. Add the broccoli florets to the boiling water and steam for 3-4 minutes or until they're tender and bright green.
3. Drain the broccoli and transfer it to a serving dish.
4. Drizzle the olive oil and fresh lemon juice over the broccoli and toss it to distribute evenly.
5. Season the Steamed Broccoli with Lemon with salt and pepper to taste.
6. Serve the Steamed Broccoli with Lemon immediately as a healthy and delicious side dish.

This recipe is suitable for the Golo Diet as it's low in calories and carbohydrates and high in fiber and nutrients. It's a great option for a quick and easy side dish to accompany any meal. Enjoy!

Sweet and Spicy Roasted Butternut Squash

Ingredients:

- 1 cup diced butternut squash
- 1/2 tbsp olive oil
- 1/2 tbsp maple syrup
- 1/2 tsp smoked paprika
- 1/4 tsp chili powder
- Salt and pepper to taste

Instructions:

1. Preheat the oven to 400°F (200°C).
2. Line a baking sheet with parchment paper or a silicone mat.
3. In a small bowl, whisk together the olive oil, maple syrup, smoked paprika, chili powder, salt, and pepper.
4. Add the diced butternut squash to the bowl and toss it in the spice mixture until it's coated evenly.
5. Spread the seasoned butternut squash in a single layer on the prepared baking sheet.
6. Roast the butternut squash for 20-25 minutes or until it's tender and caramelized.
7. Serve the Sweet and Spicy Roasted Butternut Squash immediately as a healthy and delicious side dish.

This recipe is suitable for the Golo Diet as it's low in calories and carbohydrates and high in fiber and nutrients. It's a great option for a quick and easy side dish to accompany any meal. Enjoy!

Desserts and Sweet Treats

Flourless Chocolate Cake

Ingredients:

- 1/2 ripe avocado
- 1/2 ripe banana
- 1 egg
- 1/4 cup unsweetened cocoa powder
- 1/4 cup honey
- 1/2 tsp vanilla extract
- 1/4 tsp baking soda
- Pinch of salt
- Fresh berries, for serving

Instructions:

1. Preheat the oven to 350°F (180°C).
2. In a food processor or blender, blend the avocado, banana, and egg until smooth.
3. Add the cocoa powder, honey, vanilla extract, baking soda, and salt to the food processor or blender and blend until well combined.
4. Pour the batter into a small greased baking dish.
5. Bake the Flourless Chocolate Cake for 20-25 minutes or until a toothpick inserted into the center comes out clean.

Desserts and Sweet Treats

6. Let the cake cool for a few minutes before slicing and serving.

7. Optional: top with fresh berries for added flavor and nutrition.

This recipe is suitable for the Golo Diet as it's low in refined sugar and high in healthy fats and fiber from the avocado and banana. It's a great option for a healthy and indulgent dessert. Enjoy!

Baked Applies with Cinnamon

Ingredients:

- 1 medium apple, cored
- 1/2 tbsp butter or coconut oil
- 1/2 tsp cinnamon
- 1/4 tsp nutmeg
- Pinch of salt

Instructions:

1. Preheat the oven to 350°F (180°C).
2. Place the cored apple in a baking dish.
3. In a small bowl, melt the butter or coconut oil in the microwave or on the stovetop.
4. Add the cinnamon, nutmeg, and salt to the bowl and stir until well combined.
5. Spoon the cinnamon mixture over the apple, making sure to cover the entire surface.
6. Bake the Baked Apples with Cinnamon for 20-25 minutes or until the apple is tender and the topping is caramelized.
7. Let the apple cool for a few minutes before serving.

This recipe is suitable for the Golo Diet as it's low in refined sugar and high in fiber and nutrients from the apple. It's a great option for a healthy and delicious dessert. Enjoy!

Desserts and Sweet Treats

Coconut Macaroons

Ingredients:

- 1/2 cup unsweetened shredded coconut
- 1 egg white
- 2 tbsp honey
- 1/4 tsp vanilla extract
- Pinch of salt

Instructions:

1. Preheat the oven to 350°F (180°C).
2. In a small bowl, whisk the egg white until frothy.
3. Add the honey, vanilla extract, and salt to the bowl and whisk until well combined.
4. Add the shredded coconut to the bowl and stir until it's fully coated in the egg white mixture.
5. Line a baking sheet with parchment paper.
6. Using a spoon or cookie scoop, form the coconut mixture into small mounds and place them on the prepared baking sheet.
7. Bake the Coconut Macaroons for 12-15 minutes or until they're golden brown and crispy on the outside.
8. Let the macaroons cool for a few minutes before serving.

This recipe is suitable for the Golo Diet as it's low in refined sugar and high in healthy fats and fiber from the shredded coconut. It's a great option for a healthy and satisfying dessert or snack. Enjoy!

Greek Yogurt with Honey and Nuts

Ingredients:

- 1/2 cup plain Greek yogurt

- 1 tbsp honey

- 1/4 cup mixed nuts (such as almonds, walnuts, and pecans), chopped

Instructions:

1. In a small bowl, stir together the Greek yogurt and honey until well combined.

2. Top the yogurt with the chopped mixed nuts.

3. Serve immediately.

This recipe is suitable for the Golo Diet as it's low in refined sugar and high in protein, healthy fats, and fiber from the Greek yogurt and mixed nuts. It's a great option for a healthy and satisfying breakfast or snack. Enjoy!

Mixed Berry Crumble

Ingredients:

- 1 cup mixed berries
- 1/4 cup almond flour
- 1/4 cup rolled oats
- 2 tbsp coconut oil or butter
- 1 tbsp honey
- 1/4 tsp cinnamon
- Pinch of salt

Instructions:

1. Preheat the oven to 375°F (190°C).
2. Rinse and chop the mixed berries and place them in a small baking dish.
3. In a small bowl, mix together the almond flour, rolled oats, coconut oil or butter, honey, cinnamon, and salt until it forms a crumbly mixture.
4. Sprinkle the crumble mixture evenly over the berries in the baking dish.
5. Bake the Mixed Berry Crumble for 20-25 minutes or until the topping is golden brown and the berries are soft and bubbly.
6. Let the crumble cool for a few minutes before serving.

This recipe is suitable for the Golo Diet as it's low in refined sugar and high in fiber, healthy fats, and antioxidants from the mixed berries and almond flour. It's a great option for a healthy and delicious dessert or snack. Enjoy!

Chocolate-Dipped Strawberries

Ingredients:

- 5-6 strawberries, rinsed and dried
- 1 oz dark chocolate (at least 70% cacao)
- 1 tsp coconut oil
- Optional toppings: chopped nuts, shredded coconut, or sea salt

Instructions:

1. Line a small baking sheet with parchment paper.
2. In a small microwave-safe bowl, heat the dark chocolate and coconut oil in the microwave in 15-second intervals, stirring in between, until melted and smooth.
3. Holding the stem of each strawberry, dip it into the melted chocolate, twisting it gently to coat it fully.
4. Place the chocolate-dipped strawberries on the prepared baking sheet.
5. If desired, sprinkle the strawberries with chopped nuts, shredded coconut, or a pinch of sea salt.
6. Refrigerate the Chocolate-Dipped Strawberries for 10-15 minutes or until the chocolate has hardened.
7. Serve immediately.

This recipe is suitable for the Golo Diet as it uses dark chocolate, which is low in sugar and high in antioxidants, and coconut oil, which is a healthy source of fat. It's a great option for a healthy and delicious dessert or snack. Enjoy!

Almond Butter Cookies

Ingredients:

- 1/2 cup almond butter
- 1/4 cup coconut sugar
- 1/2 tsp baking soda
- 1/4 tsp salt
- 1 egg
- 1 tsp vanilla extract

Instructions:

1. Preheat the oven to 350°F (180°C). Line a baking sheet with parchment paper.
2. In a mixing bowl, combine the almond butter, coconut sugar, baking soda, and salt. Stir until well mixed.
3. Add in the egg and vanilla extract, and mix until the dough is smooth and well combined.
4. Using a spoon, scoop the dough into 1-2 inch balls and place them onto the prepared baking sheet. Flatten them with a fork.
5. Bake for 8-10 minutes or until the edges are golden brown.
6. Remove from the oven and let the cookies cool on the baking sheet for 5 minutes before transferring them to a wire rack to cool completely.

This recipe is suitable for the Golo Diet as it's low in refined sugar and high in healthy fats and protein from the almond butter. It's a great option for a healthy and satisfying dessert or snack. Enjoy!

Desserts and Sweet Treats

Frozen Banana Bites

Ingredients:

- 1 ripe banana

- 1/4 cup dark chocolate chips (at least 70% cacao)

- 1 tsp coconut oil

- Optional toppings: chopped nuts, shredded coconut, or sea salt

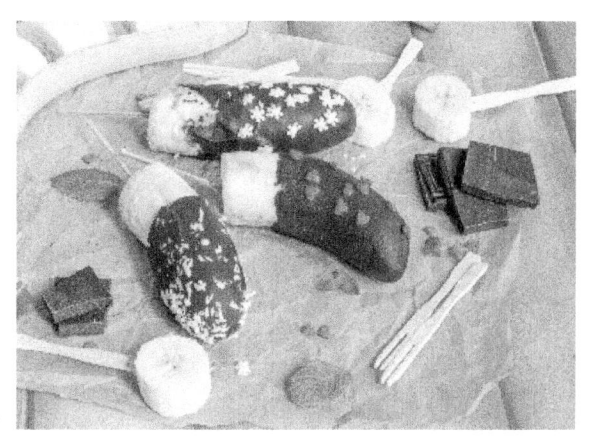

Instructions:

1. Line a small baking sheet with parchment paper.

2. Peel the banana and slice it into 1/2 inch thick rounds.

3. In a small microwave-safe bowl, heat the dark chocolate and coconut oil in the microwave in 15-second intervals, stirring in between, until melted and smooth.

4. Using a fork or toothpick, dip each banana slice into the melted chocolate, twisting it gently to coat it fully.

5. Place the chocolate-dipped banana slices on the prepared baking sheet.

6. If desired, sprinkle the banana bites with chopped nuts, shredded coconut, or a pinch of sea salt.

7. Freeze the banana bites for 1-2 hours or until fully frozen.

8. Serve immediately or store in an airtight container in the freezer for up to 1 week.

This recipe is suitable for the Golo Diet as it uses dark chocolate, which is low in sugar and high in antioxidants, and coconut oil, which is a healthy source of fat. The frozen banana bites are a great option for a healthy and satisfying dessert or snack. Enjoy!

Pumpkin Mousse

Ingredients:

- 1/2 cup pumpkin puree
- 1/4 cup plain Greek yogurt
- 1/4 cup coconut cream
- 1 tbsp honey
- 1/2 tsp vanilla extract
- 1/2 tsp cinnamon
- 1/4 tsp nutmeg
- Optional toppings: chopped nuts or whipped cream (use coconut whipped cream for a dairy-free option)

Instructions:

1. In a mixing bowl, whisk together the pumpkin puree, Greek yogurt, coconut cream, honey, vanilla extract, cinnamon, and nutmeg until well combined and smooth.
2. Divide the mixture into 2 small serving bowls or glasses.
3. Refrigerate for at least 30 minutes or until set.
4. If desired, top with chopped nuts or a dollop of whipped cream before serving.

This recipe is suitable for the Golo Diet as it's low in sugar and high in protein and healthy fats from the Greek yogurt and coconut cream. It's a great option for a healthy and satisfying dessert or snack. Enjoy!

Fruit Salad with Lime and Mint

Ingredients:

- 1 cup mixed chopped fruit
- 1 tbsp lime juice
- 1 tsp honey
- 1 tbsp chopped fresh mint leaves

Instructions:

1. In a mixing bowl, combine the chopped fruit.
2. In a small bowl, whisk together the lime juice and honey until well combined.
3. Drizzle the lime-honey mixture over the fruit and toss to coat.
4. Add the chopped fresh mint leaves and toss gently to combine.
5. Serve immediately or refrigerate for up to 2 hours before serving.

This recipe is suitable for the Golo Diet as it's low in added sugar and high in fiber and antioxidants from the mixed fruit. The lime and mint add a refreshing twist to the fruit salad. Enjoy!

Beverages

Cucumber Mint Infused Water

Ingredients:

- 1/2 cucumber, sliced

- 5-6 fresh mint leaves

- 2 cups of water

Instructions:

1. Fill a pitcher or large glass with 2 cups of water.

2. Add the sliced cucumber and fresh mint leaves to the water.

3. Stir gently to combine.

4. Let the water sit in the refrigerator for at least 1 hour to allow the flavors to infuse.

5. Serve the cucumber mint infused water over ice, garnished with additional mint leaves if desired.

This recipe is suitable for the Golo Diet as it's low in sugar and calories and helps to keep you hydrated. The cucumber and mint add a refreshing flavor to the water, making it a healthy and tasty alternative to sugary drinks. Enjoy!

Green Tea with Lemon and Ginger

Ingredients:

- 1 green tea bag
- 1 cup boiling water
- 1 tbsp fresh lemon juice
- 1 tsp grated fresh ginger
- Optional: honey or stevia to taste

Instructions:

1. Place the green tea bag in a mug and pour boiling water over it.
2. Let the tea steep for 2-3 minutes.
3. Remove the tea bag and add the fresh lemon juice and grated ginger.
4. Stir well to combine.
5. If desired, add honey or stevia to taste.
6. Serve the green tea with lemon and ginger hot or let it cool and enjoy it over ice.

This recipe is suitable for the Golo Diet as it's low in sugar and calories and contains antioxidants from the green tea, vitamin C from the lemon juice, and anti-inflammatory properties from the ginger. Enjoy this delicious and healthy drink!

Iced Coffee with Almond Milk

Ingredients:

- 1 cup brewed coffee, chilled
- 1/2 cup unsweetened almond milk
- Optional: stevia or sugar-free sweetener to taste
- Optional: ice cubes

Instructions:

1. Brew a cup of coffee and let it cool in the refrigerator or freezer until chilled.
2. In a glass, add the chilled coffee and the unsweetened almond milk.
3. If desired, add stevia or sugar-free sweetener to taste.
4. If desired, add ice cubes to the glass.
5. Stir well to combine.
6. Serve the iced coffee with almond milk cold.

This recipe is suitable for the Golo Diet as it's low in sugar and calories and contains healthy fats and protein from the almond milk. Enjoy this refreshing and delicious coffee drink!

Strawberry and Basil Lemonade

Ingredients:

- 1 cup water
- 1/4 cup fresh strawberries, sliced
- 1 tbsp fresh basil, chopped
- 1 tbsp fresh lemon juice
- Optional: honey or stevia to taste
- Optional: ice cubes

Instructions:

1. In a blender, combine the water, fresh strawberries, and fresh basil.
2. Blend until smooth.
3. In a glass, add the fresh lemon juice and the blended strawberry and basil mixture.
4. If desired, add honey or stevia to taste.
5. If desired, add ice cubes to the glass.
6. Stir well to combine.
7. Serve the strawberry and basil lemonade cold.

This recipe is suitable for the Golo Diet as it's low in sugar and calories and contains antioxidants from the strawberries and anti-inflammatory properties from the basil. Enjoy this refreshing and flavorful lemonade!

Golden Milk Latte

Ingredients:

- 1 cup unsweetened almond milk
- 1/2 tsp ground turmeric
- 1/4 tsp ground cinnamon
- 1/4 tsp ground ginger
- 1/4 tsp vanilla extract
- Optional: stevia or honey to taste

Instructions:

1. In a small pot, warm the unsweetened almond milk over medium heat until it begins to steam.
2. Add the ground turmeric, ground cinnamon, ground ginger, and vanilla extract to the pot.
3. Whisk the ingredients until well combined.
4. If desired, add stevia or honey to taste.
5. Continue to whisk the ingredients until the sweetener is dissolved and the mixture is frothy.
6. Pour the Golden Milk Latte into a mug and enjoy!

This recipe is suitable for the Golo Diet as it's low in sugar and calories and contains anti-inflammatory properties from the turmeric and ginger. Enjoy this warm and comforting latte!

Printed in Great Britain
by Amazon